Helping Children to Build Self-Esteem

of related interest:

Helping Adolescents and Adults to Build Self-Esteem
Deborah Plummer
ISBN 1 84310 185 8

Using Interactive Imagework with Children
Walking on the Magic Mountain
Deborah Plummer
ISBN 1 85302 671 9

Social Awareness Skills for Children
Marianna Csoti
ISBN 1 84310 003 7

Dream Time with Children
Learning to Dream, Dreaming to Learn
Brenda Mallon
ISBN 1 84310 014 2

Listening to Young People in School, Youth Work and Counselling
Nick Luxmoore
ISBN 1 85302 909 2

My Social Stories Book
Carol Gray
Illustrated by Sean McAndrew
ISBN 1 85302 950 5

New Perspectives on Bullying
Ken Rigby
ISBN 1 85302 872 X

Helping Children to Build Self-Esteem

A Photocopiable Activities Book

Deborah Plummer

Jessica Kingsley Publishers
London and Philadelphia

First published in the United Kingdom in 2001 by
Jessica Kingsley Publishers Ltd,
116 Pentonville Road, London
N1 9JB, England
and
400 Market Street, Suite 400
Philadelphia, PA 19106, USA

www.jkp.com

© Copyright 2001 Deborah Plummer

Reprinted twice in 2002
Fourth impression 2003
Reprinted twice 2004

Library of Congress Cataloging in Publication Data
A CIP catalog record for this book is available from the Library of Congress

British Library Cataloguing in Publication Data
A CIP catalogue record for this book is available from the British Library

ISBN 1 85302 927 0

Printed and Bound in Great Britain by
Athenaeum Press, Gateshead, Tyne and Wear

Contents

Part 3 Activity Worksheets

Acknowledgements

Some of the ideas presented here may be familiar to you, as they are based on well-established techniques for promoting self-esteem. However, most have 'developed themselves' either on the spot during therapy sessions with individual children or during the preparation and debriefing periods for more groups than it is useful for me to count! My main source of inspiration has been imagework for which I have Dina Glouberman to thank. Her creative and unique courses, her ongoing support and the support of my fellow imagework practitioners have all been nothing less than magical!

My grateful thanks go to all the children who have tried out these exercises so enthusiastically, and to my niece Alice Harper, who has patiently transformed my stick drawings into the wonderful characters and objects that appear throughout the book.

Introduction

Although the imagination is a naturally occurring and abundant resource, I did not recognize its potential as a powerful tool for change until I was in my early thirties. At that time I was searching for ways both to expand my clinical practice and to find a self-help method that resonated with my beliefs about human development. My exploration of the connections between mind and body eventually led me to courses on imagework run by Dina Glouberman. Dina, who is a psychotherapist and founder/director of the Skyros Centre, Greece, leads imagework training courses internationally. She created the term 'imagework' to describe a particular way of working with images: '…a way of tapping into, exploring, and changing the images that guide our lives' (Glouberman 1992, p.2).

As I began to use imagework regularly in my own life, its creative potential for children became increasingly obvious to me – it seemed such a natural way to help children further equip themselves to face the challenges of life. To begin with I used images in the framework of guided journeys or stories, encouraging children to interact with the characters and objects that they met and to create their own images to represent problems, dilemmas and questions. However, it soon became clear that many children would also benefit from using *brief* imagery exercises, and that they needed to engage in a wide variety of 'expansion' activities to facilitate the transition from internalized images to the practical applications of skills in everyday life.

What therefore started as a collection of therapy and homework tasks gradually grew into an activities book. The format that I have chosen is based on a blend of imagery and 'personal construct psychology' (e.g. Kelly 1955). The photocopiable handouts can be used either as a complete course or as a resource to dip into and adapt as needed. My intention is that this format will allow for flexibility in how the material is used; enabling therapists, teachers, social workers, counsellors, nurses, psychologists and other professionals to utilize the handouts and activity ideas with individuals and groups in a variety of settings. In my own work I have used the ideas presented here with children who stutter or who have mild language impairments. I also use them with children who have no specific speech or language difficulties but who are underachieving at school or have poor social skills.

Part 1 of the book includes a brief overview of imagery and self-esteem. For readers who would like to explore each of the areas in more depth I have suggested some useful texts. However, the majority of the book (Parts 2 and 3) is devoted to the practical application of the ideas.

Please note that throughout the text when referring to 'a child' the pronouns 'he' and 'she' have been used interchangeably.

Suggestions for further reading

Fransella, F. and Dalton, P. (1990) *Personal Construct Counselling in Action.* London: Sage.

Glouberman, D. (1999) *Life Choices, Life Changes: Develop Your Personal Vision with Imagework.* London: Thorsons.

Kelly, G.A. (1955) *The Psychology of Personal Constructs.* New York: Norton.

Part 1

Theoretical Background

Chapter 1

Imagery and the Process of Change

We are all able to produce internal images of one sort or another. Some people can 'see' things clearly in their imagination, others may get a sense of an image but not a clear picture. Some people have mostly auditory or feeling images. These images are a natural part of our lives and are our earliest means of making sense of the world. They form the basis of our knowledge about ourselves and others, and about our environment before we are ever able to communicate through words:

> Many of our guiding images emerge in infancy and early childhood, at a time when imagery is the dominant mode of thought, and they guide not only our thoughts but our body functioning and our whole way of being. (Glouberman 1992, p.43)

Throughout life we build up a memory bank of these internal images. Part of this is conscious, but much of it passes into our unconscious mind, stored away in the 'vaults' and yet still capable of informing our actions.

The richness and creativity of our imagination means that it is also possible to create new images that will work for us. These can replace or outweigh old stored images, formed through past experience, that are no longer useful for our self-development. Such creativity allows for the possibility of challenging old belief systems and of creating a positive future for ourselves.

Changing or challenging a stored image tends to have repercussions on other levels:

> ...imagery does seem to have a set of unique qualities which include a powerful ability to connect us with parts of us that words do not reach – in

particular, thoughts, feelings, intuitions, and body functions that are normally unconscious. (Glouberman 1992, pp.21–22)

Images 'speak' to us on a level that can be described as a meeting point between the unconscious and the conscious mind. They offer us a chance to supplement logical, analytical thinking with a more holistic view of ourselves and the world, but they do not require detailed analysis for shifts in perception to take place. It is important to remember this when helping children to use their imagination. We can encourage them to talk about their images and to talk *with* their images, but we should resist any temptation to offer our own interpretations as to what they might mean. Images are generally very personal to the individual. They should be seen in the context of where, when and how they were created, and in the light of each child's way of viewing the world. Like any insight offered by a child, images demand respect, not adult analysis!

My belief is that children with low self-esteem have what could be referred to as 'negative image patterning'. For example, an image that a child might have of herself failing in one situation interconnects with a myriad other images so that she eventually sees herself as 'a person who fails'. However, I also believe that we can help children to create new images and to develop more effective image patterns that work for them.

Providing children with the means to foster creative use of the imagination can help them to build a unified sense of their inner and outer worlds; can enable them to see events, problems and challenges from a different viewpoint; and can help them to find the way forward that is most appropriate for their individual needs. The resultant ability to make more informed choices in life will surely lead to a feeling of control, and will contribute to higher self-esteem, more effective learning and more fulfilling relationships. In fact, the imagination is a natural resource that none of us can afford to ignore!

Suggestions for further reading

Bettelheim, B. (1978) *The Uses of Enchantment.* Harmondsworth: Penguin.

Glouberman, D. (1999) *Life Choices, Life Changes: Develop Your Personal Vision with Imagework.* London: Thorsons.

Johnson, R. (1989) *Inner Work: Using Dreams and Active Imagination for Personal Growth.* New York: HarperSanFrancisco.

Plummer, D. (1998) *Using Interactive Imagework with Children: Walking on the Magic Mountain.* London: Jessica Kingsley Publishers.

Chapter 2

Self-Esteem –
The Foundation of Learning

What is self-esteem? How does it develop? What happens when self-esteem is low? These questions have been addressed in numerous research articles and self-help books over the last 20 years or so, reflecting the recognition that self-esteem is a primary factor in the building and maintenance of social and emotional well-being. A child who has a healthy level of self-esteem is more likely to achieve at his full potential and form successful relationships than the child who suffers from acute feelings of lack of self-worth.

Self-esteem is about feeling lovable *and* feeling competent. If you have been drawn to this book, then you have probably had many experiences of working with children with low self-esteem. Some of these children appear to place little value on their abilities and often deny their successes. They find it difficult to set goals and to problem-solve. Many give up trying and consequently perform well below their academic and social capabilities. Their self-limiting beliefs become a self-fulfilling prophecy. If a child has low self-esteem, a hundred people can tell him that he has done well but he will believe the one who says he needs to do better.

There are also many children who *do* achieve at or near their academic potential but have a constant fear of failure and a drive for perfection that may preclude creativity and experimentation. Such a child may set unrealistically high personal goals, thus constantly confirming to himself that he is 'no good' each time that he experiences failure. Self-esteem, it appears, is not dependent on measurable success but comes from a strong sense of self-worth that can cope with both failures *and* successes.

How does self-esteem develop? To begin with, a young child will rely heavily on external means to confirm his self-worth and competence. He looks to the significant people in his life (e.g. parents, grandparents, teachers) to show him that he is loved and approved of. Virginia Satir, family therapist, writes:

> An infant coming into the world has no past, no experience in handling himself, no scale on which to judge his own worth. He must rely on the experiences he has with the people around him and the messages they give him about his worth as a person. (Satir 1972, p.24)

The way that a child interprets verbal and non-verbal messages from others plays an important part in this. By non-verbal I mean such aspects as facial expression, body language and even the way that we structure a child's environment. It has been suggested that in face-to-face interactions, 55 per cent of the emotional meaning of a message is expressed through facial, postural and gestural means, and 38 per cent of the emotional meaning is transmitted through the tone of voice (e.g. Mehrabian, reported in Nowicki and Duke 1992). When we talk we talk with the whole of us. If our messages are ambiguous or inconsistent, a child will tend to believe the body language rather than the spoken words.

If a child's early experiences have been primarily positive with regard to this building of self-esteem, then eventually he will be able to internalize the feelings of self-worth and rely less and less on others for approval and confirmation that he is 'OK'. A child who believes in himself and who has developed a degree of self-reliance is more likely to be able to cope with life's inevitable difficulties. However, a child who remains dependent on external sources for the maintenance of self-esteem will find misfortunes much more difficult to handle and will invariably use another's actions and reactions to define himself.

> Such a child will develop into an adult who will continue to feel that he has to be successful, or good, or approved of by everyone, if he is to retain any sense of his own value…as though they were entirely dependent for maintaining their self-esteem upon the successes of whatever enterprise was currently engaging them, without taking into account past blessings or future possibilities. (Storr 1989, p.96)

Elements of self-esteem

My observations and clinical experience indicate that there are seven main elements that form the foundation for social and emotional health and thereby lead to high self-esteem. The interaction is reciprocal – high levels of self-esteem will enable the consolidation and growth of these seven elements. With the right support and environment, the seeds of these elements sown in childhood should continue to grow and, hopefully, to flourish through adulthood.

I have addressed aspects of each element in Sections II–VIII of the activities but these divisions are, of course, somewhat false since in reality all areas are interdependent. I have not, therefore, presented them in any hierarchical or developmental order.

Self-knowledge

- Developing a sense of security in terms of a strong sense of self: an understanding of who 'I' am and where I fit into the social world around me.

- Understanding differences and commonalities – how I am different from others in looks and character and how I can also have things in common with others. How people can act in different ways according to the situation that they are in.

Self and others

- Knowing how relationships function, in particular being able to develop and maintain my own identity as a separate person while still recognizing the natural *inter*dependence of relationships.

- Understanding the difficulties inherent in relationships and in learning to co-operate with each other.

- Seeing things from another person's perspective and developing an understanding of how they might see me. Learning respect and tolerance for other people's views.

- Understanding my emotions and being aware of the ways in which I express them.

- Knowing that I can choose *how* to express emotions appropriately, rather than deny or repress them or act in an inappropriate way.

- Recognizing other people's emotions and being able to distinguish my feelings from those of others.

Self-acceptance

- Knowing my own strengths and recognizing areas that I find difficult and may want to work on.

- Accepting that it is natural to make mistakes and that this is often how we learn best.

- Knowing that I am doing the best that I can with the knowledge and skills currently available to me.

- Feeling OK about my physical body.

Self-reliance

- Knowing how to take care of myself.

- Understanding that life is often difficult but there are lots of things that I can do for myself to help smooth the path.

- Building a measure of independence and self-motivation.

- Being able to self-monitor and adjust my actions, feelings and thoughts according to realistic assessments of my progress.

- Believing that I have mastery over my life and can meet challenges as and when they arise.

Self-expression

- Understanding how we communicate with each other, not just with words but also through facial expression, body posture, intonation, the clothes we wear, etc.

- Learning to 'read the signals' beyond the words so that I can understand others more successfully and also express myself more fully and congruently.

- Developing creativity in self-expression. Recognizing and celebrating the unique ways in which we each express who we are.

Self-confidence

- Knowing that my opinions, thoughts and actions have value and that I have the right to express them.

- Knowing that I have the right to be me and that I make a difference.

- Developing a creative approach to solving problems and being confident enough in my own abilities to be able to experiment with different methods of problem-solving and to be flexible enough to alter strategies if needed.

- Being able to accept challenges and to make choices.

Self-awareness

- Developing the ability to be focused in the here and now, rather than absorbed in negative thoughts about the past or future. This includes an awareness of my feelings as they arise.

- Knowing what I am capable of, and learning to set realistic yet challenging goals.

- Understanding that emotional, mental and physical change is a natural part of my life.

- Understanding that I have some control in *how* I change and develop.

- Being secure enough in myself to be able to develop strategies for coping successfully with the unexpected.

This list may seem huge and somewhat daunting but it is not an impossible task to create an environment where children have every chance of developing these elements to some degree.

In summary, I believe that there is much that can be done to help children to build and maintain self-esteem in the face of life's many challenges, and to help the child whose fragile sense of self-esteem is already bruised. The development of self-esteem is intimately bound up with a child's experiences in life. Adults, of course, play a vital role in this. Adult communication with children therefore needs to be clear, unambiguous, non-judgemental and unconditional. We need to show that we respect their opinions and value their participation, that we believe they have a significant role to play and that we are interested in them as individuals. We need to encourage them to recognize their successes, to allow them to work at their own level, to set realistic goals and to self-evaluate successfully. Not a small task by any means, but one that will be infinitely rewarding for those who incorporate this way of being into their daily interactions with children.

Suggestions for further reading

Faber, A. and Mazlish, E. (1982) *How to Talk So Kids Will Listen and Listen So Kids Will Talk.* New York: Avon.

Satir, V. (1972) *Peoplemaking.* London: Souvenir Press.

Chapter 3

Working within the School Curriculum

Much has been written in recent years about the importance of creating a classroom atmosphere that supports self-esteem. This reflects an understanding of education as encompassing cognitive, emotional, spiritual and physical development, rather than just academic achievement alone. Gurney writes: 'It is possible to argue, and I certainly do, that self-esteem is the core concept upon which a revitalized curriculum should be based.' He goes on to say: 'The State of California in 1975 identified self-esteem as a major goal in education, ranking with reading, writing and arithmetic. The argument in this text is that self-esteem is *the* prime goal for education' (Gurney 1988, p.78).

Teachers are in an excellent position to support the self-esteem of the children in their care, but for those children who are struggling to find themselves at all worthy of love and respect it will be a lengthy task requiring a consistent and dedicated approach. A classroom environment that encourages active discussion and shows children that their contributions are valued and respected will go a long way towards aiding the process. Circle-times, which are an established routine in many classes, do much to address this need for children's learning to be set in the context of a whole-person approach. Most of the activities described in this book (Part 2) can be incorporated into circle-time sessions. Where these are not already in existence, teachers will be able to use the format I have outlined to create a regular time slot for this type of interactive sharing and learning if they want to. There is enough material here to span a full academic year if sessions are brief and shorter activities and ideas are incorporated into the natural routines of the day.

The activity sheets (Part 3) can be adapted for different age groups and ability levels and will fulfil many literacy and PHSE learning objectives for Key Stages 1 and 2. There is a deliberate mixture of listening, speaking, reading, writing and drawing, as well as individual and group work.

Increasingly, teachers have developed considerable skills in devising approaches to learning that can be adapted to address the wide diversity of individual needs within their classes. However, research in this area has not come up with a definitive answer to the question of which comes first – high self-esteem or academic achievement. The two are, undoubtedly, closely interlinked. And the relationship may be a reciprocal one:

> Some writers regard self-esteem as a threshold variable...that is to say it may not be as strong or significant in its effect on academic performance when it is at an average or above average levels but it seriously inhibits persistence, confidence and academic performance when the child's self-esteem is at a low level. It is therefore argued that, whatever one's assumptions about the direction of causality between low self-esteem and academic achievement, in the case of markedly low self-esteem, one *must* seek to enhance that first before undertaking any remedial teaching. (Gurney 1988, p.57)

As inconclusive as the research might be, the important point to remember is the heavy reliance that young children place on positive feedback from significant others in their lives (see p.17) – every look, comment, action has potential to contribute to their concept of who they are and their feeling of value. We cannot therefore assume that a child with low self-esteem will suddenly be able to value herself through internalizing her academic achievement. Her environment and the way that she interprets this will have a huge part to play.

This book offers a wide selection of ideas to aid the process of supporting self-esteem. The main aim of the activities is, of course, to help children to develop the seven areas outlined in Chapter 2. However, within this framework, the activity sheets and expansion activities also aim to:

- foster an atmosphere where children can be actively engaged in the learning process

- encourage spontaneity and creativity

- help focus thought processes

- encourage expansion of vocabulary knowledge

- develop higher-level thinking skills

- provide an opportunity to develop and practise organizational and self-monitoring skills

- encourage tolerance and respect of other people's ideas

- provide a vehicle for positive interaction with peers.

The structure provided by having a general theme throughout the sessions, together with repeated patterns of imagery, will help children to establish a familiar format for problem-solving and goal-setting, which they can then be guided to use in a variety of lessons. In this way children can be encouraged in the development of their imaginative and creative skills to support their learning in all areas of academic and social development.

Suggestions for further reading

Gurney, P. (1988) *Self-Esteem in Children with Special Educational Needs*. London and New York: Routledge.

Robinson, G. and Maines, B. (1989) 'A Self-Concept Approach to Dealing with Pupils.' In R. Evans (ed) *Special Educational Needs 'Policy and Practice'*. Oxford: Blackwell Education in association with National Association for Remedial Education.

Chapter 4

The Child with Speech
and Language Difficulties

Estimates suggest that between 14 per cent and 20 per cent of pre-school children have delayed or deviant speech or language. This percentage decreases with age. Studies of problems in speech, language, voice and fluency (e.g. stuttering) in school-aged children suggest an average prevalence rate of 5 per cent (Royal College of Speech and Language Therapists 1998).

Self-esteem can so easily be affected when children have to cope with specific difficulties such as speech and language delay or disorder. In Chapter 2 I talked about how we convey messages through the 'whole' of us. Our speech is naturally full of ambiguities and often our verbal messages don't match our non-verbal communication. We expect children to learn the subtleties of our ways of communicating through listening and observation, rather than through specific teaching; but the child with speech and language difficulties may find this extremely difficult and can often misinterpret messages. Mistakes in interpreting and using non-verbal communication can lead to a child feeling isolated and confused.

The child with a speech or language difficulty will have had countless experiences of not understanding what is being said to him or others not understanding what he is saying. He may have had people look at him blankly, ask 'what did he say?' over his head or, worst of all, laugh at his speech efforts or tease him. The child who stutters, for example, is often acutely aware of the effect that his struggle to speak may be having on some of his listeners – effects ranging from impatience to mirth, sympathy and sometimes physical tension. Each of these experiences has potential to erode his self-esteem.

Furthermore, although children with communication difficulties may well have average or above-average intelligence, others (adults as well as peers) often view them as 'not very bright'. Once this concept has been formed and transmitted to the child he may become resigned to it or give up trying to compete and begin instead to underachieve because this fits in with how he is expected to behave. Even a relatively mild communication impairment can thereby have far-reaching effects on self-esteem, interpersonal relationships and classroom performance.

Not only do children take note of other people's comments, they also need to develop the ability to use language in a way that helps them to define their successes and limitations. For those who have limited speech or language skills, 'the inability to negotiate with others verbally, to stake one's claim to attributes that others are ignoring, or to deny an attribution that seems unfair, for example, means that the elaboration of self-concepts is impeded' (Dalton 1994, p.3).

When devising a self-esteem 'programme' we therefore need to take account of the fact that language primarily performs a social function. Many of the activities offered here are aimed at promoting this social use of language. In particular, conversation skills (starting, maintaining and ending a conversation), internal responses (identification and expression of emotions) and descriptions of objects. Studies indicate that these areas can significantly improve with therapy (e.g. Richardson and Klecan-Aker 2000).

Although I have run groups specifically for children with speech and language difficulties, I believe that including these children in whole-class activities based on raising self-esteem has potential to have an equal, if not more profound, effect. They will be able to see that they are not the only ones who have doubts and uncertainties about their abilities; they are not the only ones who have to develop 'strategies' to cope with teasing and so on. Such joint activities will also help others in the group to appreciate the diversity of ways in which we communicate with each other.

By specifically giving children the chance to learn to read signals more accurately and to understand more about themselves and their abilities, we can support and encourage their learning and their self-esteem. The repetitive nature of the exercises presented here is intended to particularly help in this process. All the activity sheets can be adapted to suit varying levels of language and general ability.

Suggestions for further reading

Dalton, P. (1994) *Counselling People with Communication Problems.* London: Sage.

Fleming, P., Miller, C. and Wright, J. (1997) *Speech and Language Difficulties in Education: Approaches to Collaborative Practice for Teachers and Speech and Language Therapists.* Bicester: Winslow Press.

Chapter 5

Transfer and Maintenance of Skills

If a child does not develop a strong sense of her own worth then eventually even praise and encouragement fails to outweigh the negative effects of her previous experiences. She may begin to misinterpret what people say and do in order for new experiences to continue to 'fit' her negative self-concept. The continuance of this pattern is by no means inevitable, however. If the feeling of lack of worth is indeed something that has been learned then it can surely be unlearned: 'The possibility for this learning lasts from birth to death, so it is never too late. At any point in a person's life he can begin to feel better about himself' (Satir 1972, p.27).

The process is ongoing and self-perpetuating. Think of self-esteem levels as being like a large reservoir – man-made but needing a conducive environment and plenty of rain to be able to fulfil its purpose of providing a constant water supply. Once a child experiences a greater depth of understanding, knows more about who she is and how the world works in actuality rather than just theory, then gradually she can top up her own reservoir of self-esteem. Maybe there will be dry spells. Maybe there will be some areas of the reservoir that are more prone to shallow levels or invasion by noxious algae! These may need careful maintenance and occasional shoring up or cleaning out. For example, a child might feel good about her ability to run fast but lack the confidence to join the local athletics club. Is it her fear of meeting others? Fear of competition? Fear of failure? Fear of winning? Whatever it is, it can be addressed through exploration and creative problem-solving and by drawing on more abundant areas of the reservoir.

A child is most likely to be able to maintain progress if she:

- has support and encouragement from others

- knows from the start what might make things difficult

- sets realistic yet challenging goals, and takes one small step at a time

- takes time to reap the benefits of the goals she has already achieved

- gives herself treats and rewards (i.e. does not always rely on others to notice and praise her successes)

- understands that failure is part of success!

The suggested expansion activities are important in helping children to continue to strengthen their self-esteem, but the process is 'organic'. The ideas will hopefully also give them the means to support their learning and their journey towards adulthood.

The imagination is a powerful tool, and I believe that children can be encouraged to use this natural resource in a positive and highly effective way. As adults we can play a huge part in facilitating this process. If you decide to follow this route with an individual child or a group of children then I am sure that you will find that the techniques eventually become 'second nature' – you can encourage children to 'image' problems, decisions, dilemmas and feelings. You can offer images if it seems appropriate – 'when you were really angry with Sam just now, I got this image of a tiger that had been hurt. Is that how you felt?' 'This problem seems like a huge lump of rock to me – we just can't seem to shift it. What could we do about this rock?' Remember that images don't need to enter analysis! It is better to observe and explore images rather than try to analyse or decode them. Simply talking about them in this way can often enable a child to see solutions or can precipitate a shift in perception where none seemed possible before.

Suggestion for further reading

Glouberman, D. (1999) *Life Choices, Life Changes: Develop Your Personal Vision with Imagework.* London: Thorsons.

Chapter 6

Notes for Facilitators

Throughout this part of the book I have made repeated references to the role that adults play in helping children to build self-esteem. Wherever possible I run workshops for primary carers alongside the work that I do with the children. These workshops are aimed at highlighting not only appropriate strategies for use with children but also methods of building and maintaining our own self-esteem. If a person feels OK about herself she is much more likely to be supportive, congruent, accepting and nurturing to children. Carl Rogers formulated a general hypothesis that he believed is valid for all human relationships:

If I can create a relationship characterised on my part:

by a genuineness and transparency, in which I am my real feelings;

by warm acceptance of and prizing of the other person as a separate individual;

by a sensitive ability to see his world and himself as he sees them;

Then the other individual in the relationship:

will experience and understand aspects of himself which previously he has repressed;

will find himself becoming better integrated, more able to function effectively;

will become more similar to the person he would like to be;

will be more self-directing and self-confident;

will become more of a person, more unique and more self-expressive;

will be more understanding, more acceptant of others;

will be able to cope with the problems of life more adequately and more comfortably. (Rogers 1961, pp.37–38)

Creating space and time for ourselves and strengthening our own feelings of self-worth is vital for our well-being and provides a powerful role model for children. (See Appendix D.)

Organizing the activities

Activity sheets

You will find separate notes for each of the activity sheets. These outline the aims and offer ideas on how to present the activities. I have occasionally quoted the experiences of some of the children I have seen for therapy. Their names and personal details have been altered but their comments and images are genuine.

The activities are divided into eight sections around the theme of collecting precious treasure for a magician's treasure chest. The sections can be used in conjunction with the exercises to be found in *Using Interactive Imagework with Children* (Plummer 1998) but can also stand on their own. If you are only intending to use a limited selection you will still need to include the relevant introductory sheet for each section that you choose.

Most of the sheets can be adapted for discussion or drawing for those who struggle with writing, and there are plenty of very practical activities. In preference, I would encourage children to draw as many of the images as possible, especially those children who do not think that they are able to draw well. You might also offer to be a secretary and let children dictate what they want to say if resources permit.

Brainstorms

The idea of the brainstorms is to accept all ideas to begin with, allowing each child to contribute as much as possible without fear of judgement or 'getting it wrong'. When enough ideas have been gathered, the next stage is to encourage objective analysis (e.g. 'So, if you did this, what would happen then? How do you think you would feel?') and then to come to a consensus about the most useful ideas.

Expansion activities

These expansion activities are an integral part of the process of using imagery. They are important because they help children to connect the inner world of images to the outer world of the here and now, and in this way to gradually integrate what they have learnt into their lives. I recommend using as many of the expansion activities as possible and involving the children in inventing some for themselves.

Working with a group

Whether you are setting up a group for the first time or you are working with an established group or class there are some general principles that need to be observed for the activities to work successfully.

New groups require time spent in getting to know each other. It is important to build up your own repertoire of group 'gelling' games so that the children will feel relaxed about sharing their ideas and taking part in co-operative activities. See, for example, *Social Skills and the Speech Impaired* (Rustin and Kuhr 1989).

It is useful to establish a set of group 'rules', and to remind the group of these periodically if needed. Such rules might include the following:

- Only one person talks at a time.

- Don't talk to other children during the imagery exercises.

- Respect other people's pictures and ideas.

- There is no such thing as a wrong image.

Whatever children produce as a result of these activities, there should not, of course, be any judgement made in terms of achievement. Although some children may need guidance to help them to participate in a co-operative and creative dialogue with their peers and with the adult who is structuring the session, nothing that is said or produced during this time can ever be 'wrong'. It is important that children understand this rule right from the start so that they feel comfortable about making contributions. Children are very used to hearing themselves talked about, especially in therapy or classroom exchanges between professionals and parents. Sometimes, however, it is appropriate for children to be able to say things openly and to know that the information will not be passed on (except, of course, in relation to child protection issues). Respecting a child's contributions can so easily include asking permission to share their work and ideas with others, rather than assuming that it is OK to do so.

Virginia Satir writes:

> Feelings of worth can only flourish in an atmosphere where individual differences are appreciated, mistakes are tolerated, communication is open, and rules are flexible – the kind of atmosphere that is found in a nurturing family. (Satir 1972, p.26)

I can think of no better maxim to take on board in the running of a self-esteem group!

Imagery exercises

Many of the activity sheets involve the children in creating their own images to represent various ideas and feelings. If you would like to explore this further then more detailed guidelines on how to facilitate longer imagery exercises can be found in my earlier book *Using Interactive Imagework with Children* (pp.59–67).

Using storybooks

One of the main attractions of using storybooks to help children to develop self-awareness and appropriate coping strategies is that they are one step removed from reality, such that it is possible to explore issues and emotions in a feeling of safety. As with individual images, it is important not to interpret stories for children because the interpretations are so personal. If a child has taken a liking to a particular story, it will usually be for a reason that he may not yet have realized. Bettelheim, for example, suggests that some fairy tales get across to the child the idea that 'struggle against severe difficulties in life is unavoidable, is an intrinsic part of human existence – but that if one does not shy away, but steadfastly meets unexpected and often unjust hardships, one masters all obstacles and at the end emerges victorious' (Bettelheim 1978, p.8).

I have suggested a variety of children's storybooks to supplement the activity sheets (Appendix F). These are primarily for the younger age range (6–8). For older or more able children, books such as those by Jacqueline Wilson contain a wealth of insights into coping with difficulties. All the books listed were available at the time of writing this, but children's books tend to go out of print fairly quickly. So it is worth doing regular trawls of bookshops to find suitable stories.

Materials

These are the basic materials you will need for the expansion activities (each section also has a list of any additional materials required for specific activities):

- a flip chart or whiteboard and pens
- large poster-sized paper for joint collages
- glue
- scissors
- coloured pencils/felt tips
- a children's dictionary.

A final thought

Helping children to build self-esteem is not the same as encouraging a reluctant acceptance of 'this is who I am'. Nor is it the same as encouraging bragging or aggression ('I'm OK and you're not'). The opposite of low self-esteem might quite simply be 'a quiet pleasure in being one's self' (Rogers 1961, p.87). This is the gift that we can offer to children in our care: whether it is a timely smile, a few words of support or a full self-esteem course – you can make a difference.

Suggestions for further reading

Dwivedi, K.N. (ed) (1997) *The Therapeutic Use of Stories*. London and New York: Routledge.

Rogers, C. (1961) *On Becoming a Person: A Therapist's View of Psychotherapy*. London: Constable.

Satir, V. (1972) *Peoplemaking*. London: Souvenir Press.

References

Bettelheim, B. (1978) *The Uses of Enchantment.* Harmondsworth: Penguin.

Dalton, P. (1994) *Counselling People with Communication Problems.* London: Sage.

Glouberman, D. (1992) *Life Choices and Life Changes through Imagework.* London: The Aquarian Press.

Gurney, P. (1988) *Self-Esteem in Children with Special Educational Needs.* London and New York: Routledge.

Kelly, G.A. (1955) *The Psychology of Personal Constructs.* New York: Norton.

Nowicki, S. and Duke, M. (1992) *Helping the Child Who Doesn't Fit In.* Atlanta, GA: Peachtree Publishers.

Plummer, D. (1998) *Using Interactive Imagework with Children: Walking on the Magic Mountain.* London: Jessica Kingsley Publishers.

Richardson, K. and Klecan-Aker, J.S. (2000) 'Teaching Pragmatics to Language-Learning Disabled Children: A Treatment Outcome Study.' *Child Language Teaching and Therapy 16*, 23–42.

Rogers, C. (1961) *On Becoming a Person: A Therapist's View of Psychotherapy.* London: Constable.

Royal College of Speech and Language Therapists (1998) *Clinical Guidelines by Consensus for Speech and Language Therapists.* London: Author.

Rustin, L. and Kuhr, A. (1989) *Social Skills and the Speech Impaired.* London: Taylor and Francis.

Satir, V. (1972) *Peoplemaking.* London: Souvenir Press.

Storr, A. (1989) *Solitude.* London: Fontana.

Part 2

Instructions for Self-Esteem Activities

I

Getting Started
(STARS and EMERALDS)

Stars

Aims of this section

- to introduce the concept of images

- to establish group reward systems

- to identify individual goals

Additional materials

- coloured paper for making stars

- small box or bowl

- suitable materials, such as A4 card and treasury tags, for making individual folders

- hole punch

- glitter and stickers or alternatives for decorating folders

Activity worksheets

1. WHAT ARE IMAGES? (P.95)

This introductory sheet can be used as a basis for a group discussion. Allow each child the chance to contribute an idea that he feels came from his imagination.

Compare and contrast the images that people have. Talk about all the different *types* of image that we can have. For example, some will be like pictures, some will be sounds (like imagining a conversation or a tune in your head), some will be feeling or sensation images (like imagining the feel of velvet or mud).

2. FINDING SOME MAGIC (P.96)

Read this sheet together and talk about what it means. Encourage children to put forward their own ideas and to suggest other things that could be 'magic treasure'. Sunil (11), for example, came up with 'respecting others' as being an important treasure to have.

3. MY PERSONAL RECORD OF ACHIEVEMENTS (P.97)

For a long time I used stars and stickers for rewards in the groups that I ran, believing that children needed some physical confirmation that they were managing to achieve their targets. However, the drawback to this was that it invariably became a competition with much counting and recounting of who had managed to get the most of the treasured stickers. Children would actually come and ask me for another sticker 'because I've just kept good eye contact when I asked you'! The more wily amongst them would assure other therapists in the group that I had told them to go claim a sticker from them!

In the end I came up with a slightly different system. I use the stars printed on pp.97–98. Children are told that when *everyone* has achieved a certain number of stars there will be an award ceremony. To avoid individuals being singled out by their peers as trailing behind, I make sure that everyone more or less keeps pace with their stars (although they may be rewarded for very diverse reasons). I also encourage children to point out to me when they think other members of the group have done particularly well in working towards their targets.

The praise that you write in the stars needs to be as specific as possible. 'Well done' has much less of an impact than 'I can see that you have put a lot of thought into your picture. You have used some really interesting shapes and colours' or 'Your "problem" picture really shows me what it must feel like to stutter. This is what I call artistic.' This may be too wordy for some, but I have watched children reading their stars with broad smiles and mutter such things as 'cool' whereas their response to briefer, non-descriptive praise has been neutral or fleeting at best.

Talk about the meaning of the word 'achievement' and then let children look it up in a dictionary if needed. Make sure that everyone has thought of one recent achievement to write in his or her first star. Share these in the group. This can be done in several ways. For example:

- Celebrate the achievement in some way, e.g. a round of applause as each one is read out.

- Split the group into pairs so that they can read out each other's achievements.

- Photocopy the stars or get the children to make separate ones. Re-write their achievements and put them on a wall poster with each child's name underneath.

(See expansion activities for this section.)

Encourage children to be specific about their own achievements (see comments on praise earlier). For example: 'I scored two goals last week in the school football match' or 'I made up an imaginative story about _____'.

4. THINGS I WOULD LIKE TO ACHIEVE (P.99)

Do this as a brainstorm either with the whole group or in smaller groups, depending on numbers. Allow time for children to write out their own ideas from the joint list.

Expansion activities

Each child makes a paper star and writes on it one thing that they enjoy doing (anonymously). Put all the stars in a box or bowl. Take out one at a time and read it. Each child (or at least five or six if you are running a large group) completes the sentence as though she had written it herself, giving a reason for enjoying the activity. Children may need encouragement to think of reasons other than 'because I'm good at it'!

Patrick (9) completed the sentence 'I enjoy playing the keyboard' with 'because I have wobbly hands' (he explained that this meant he could move his fingers very fast!).

This exercise encourages children to recognize and be accepting of the range of activities that other people enjoy, and to think about *why* they might enjoy them. It also gives them the chance to find out a little about any interests they might have in common and to think about some new activities to try for themselves.

Ask the owner of each star to reveal her identity and then ask for a show of hands as to who else likes the same thing. Similar stars obviously don't need to be completed in the same way but should be read out and returned to their owners. All the stars could then be mounted on one large 'sky' picture and displayed on the wall.

Note: Spend time making and decorating the folders ready for all the activity sheets. I have found that children usually take more care of their folders if they make their own than if they are provided with one.

EMERALDS

Aims of this section

- to explore imagery and the basic imagework format
- to introduce or expand on the concept of awareness of others
- to introduce the idea that what we think affects how we feel
- to set up an appropriate format for discussion, according to age and ability levels of the group

Additional materials

No additional materials are required for this section.

Activity worksheets

1. IMAGINING (P.100)

Read the exercise 'Think of a chocolate cake' slowly with plenty of pauses for the children really to explore the images. Whenever possible, ask for verbal feedback while you are doing imagery exercises. This will encourage children actually to *do* the exercise rather than just sit with their eyes closed! For example, when you say 'what does it (the cake) look like?', the group can be asked to describe the sort of chocolate cake they are imagining. Validate the responses by repeating back what you have heard the child say or by making some appropriate sound (Mmmmmm!). The interaction might go something like:

> 'You see the cake on a big plate... Would anyone like to say what their chocolate cake looks like?'

> 'It's got smarties on.'

> 'Simon's cake has smarties.'

> 'Squidgy.'

> 'Mmmm – a squidgy cake for Craig.'

When you have finished the exercise, discuss similarities and differences in the responses. Be sure to reassure children that there is no right or wrong answer. If anyone seems unable to 'see' images that's OK. In my experience, however, children are usually very quick to produce visual images.

2. TALKING CATS (P.101)

Discuss how it is usually fairly easy to imagine something that we are familiar with. If we do something regularly, we stop thinking about it too much after a while and just do it! When something new is about to happen we often imagine what it might be like. We can also imagine things that we know will never happen at all. This leads on to the next exercise.

3A. BECOMING A CAT (P.102)

3B. BEING A CAT (P.103)

I have suggested that the children dictate what they want to say about being a cat, but this is obviously only possible if you have a group of able writers or enough helpers to act as 'secretaries'. Alternatively, discuss sheet 3a in the group and expand on the vocabulary. Give sheet 3b to do individually or as a 'do at home' activity.

Expansion activities

(a) Read a story about the imagination (e.g. *And to Think That I Saw It on Mulberry Street* by Dr Seuss).

(b) Talk about what it would be like to be different animals.

(c) Set the children the task of finding out about emeralds. What colour are they? Where are they found? What are they used for?

(d) Choose some famous people and talk about what it would be like to be them. What sort of day would they have? Where would they live? What would they eat for breakfast? What would they wear?

(e) Invite the children to choose someone important in their life (parent, brother, sister, friend, etc.) and write about what they think would be a typical day for them or draw some things that they would do, wear, eat, etc.

These last two activities encourage not only use of the imagination but also awareness and acceptance of others.

II

Who Am I? (RUBIES)

Aims of this section

- to explore the concept of 'me' and 'not me'

- to understand how people are different and alike

- to introduce the idea that change is possible

- to encourage children to celebrate who they are

Additional materials

- enough hand mirrors for children to share

- silver paper or suitable alternative for making a 'magic mirror' (see expansion activities)

- a cloth or cloak to use for story telling (see expansion activities)

Activity worksheets

INTRODUCTORY PAGE (P.105)

It is important for every child to have all the relevant introductory pages, even if you don't plan to use all the activity sheets in each section. Talk about how the picture in the mirror might change. For example, the child may have a different expression, be wearing different clothes or a crown made up of the jewels being collected, or perhaps he will be holding something or doing something that shows what he has been learning.

1. THE MAGIC MIRROR (P.106)

Use photos, or look in hand mirrors, and draw self-portraits. This exercise encourages physical self-awareness. The magic mirror can be used for more than physical aspects, however. It appears at the end of each section where it can be used to help children to identify some of the changes they are making. See note to the introductory page (above).

2. IF I WERE AN ANIMAL (P.107)

This exercise uses one of the basic formats of imagework (Glouberman, 1992) – *becoming* the image in order to find out more about it. This might also help you to gain more insight into how the children perceive themselves or how they would *like* to be.

Read the passage out to the group slowly to give them time to think about it. If you are running a relatively small group, ask for verbal feedback: 'Would anyone like to tell me what animal they are?' (See notes for EMERALDS activity sheet 1 (p.41).) This encourages a feeling of connection between group members and will help you to know what's going on. It also gives more time to those who need to explore images more deeply or are having problems getting an image in the first place. Invariably, the group will not all be working at the same pace. Move on when it feels right to do so.

In large groups, when you are waiting for children to produce their own images, ask them to raise a finger when they have got an image, rather than asking them to call out. There is certainly no 'right' or 'wrong' way for a child to do imagework. Positive encouragement may help her to verbalize what she is experiencing but it is important not to insist that she shares something with you if she doesn't want to. I recommend that you allow your own images to emerge while you are reading, as this will help you to pace the instructions.

When you have completed the exercise make a joint list of the descriptive words that the children used.

3. DESCRIBING PEOPLE (P.108)

Brainstorm descriptive words and phrases. Write them all on a flip chart or whiteboard. The only rule is that there should be no 'evaluative' words (i.e. these are objective descriptions not judgements). Talk about how people are unlikely to change some physical features from one day to the next but can change other aspects (e.g. length of hair). Other things (e.g. how they act, feel, dress) can change from moment to moment. Someone who is described as thoughtful might sometimes do something that is NOT thoughtful! Most people, however, have a 'usual' way of being. The descriptions discussed don't all need to be positive. It is important for children to realize that feeling unhappy, grumpy, etc. is OK sometimes.

See also SILVER activity sheets 3 and 4 and the accompanying notes on feelings (p.54).

4. MY GROUP (P.109)

This activity sheet needs to be followed up by discussion in the group. This will help to promote not only group identity but also individual self-esteem. Talk about how it is possible to think that someone feels a certain way but that may not be how they see themselves. For example, a child might appear to be very clever but he might think that he is *not* clever compared to an older brother or sister.

You might suggest that each child 'collects' three descriptions that he likes from what others have written about him and writes these next to his first magic mirror picture. These descriptive words or phrases could also be used to start off activity sheet 5.

5. THIS IS ME (P.110)

See note for activity sheet 3 in this section.

Encourage decorations on this activity sheet!

Invite the children to read out their own descriptions in large or small groups. Start with 'My name is _____. This is how I would like to be described.'

Alternatively, read out a selection (with permission from the children) and see if the rest of the group can guess who is being described.

6. I AM ME (P.111)

Self-characterization promotes greater awareness of self and others. It is based on an idea developed by personal construct psychologists and therapists.

Looking through the completed sheets will help you to pick out important themes in how the children see themselves, what worries them, what they enjoy doing, etc. Some children find this exercise extremely difficult, having little idea of how others might see them, or indeed how they see themselves. They may need some prompts in the form of questions, such as: 'What would your best friend say about the way that you _____?'

7. EVERYONE IS DIFFERENT (P.112)

Invite fantastical answers to this!

> *A group of boys who stutter (9–12 years old) were asked to do this as a homework activity. Almost all of them wrote that if everyone was the same then we would all be fluent and no one would be teased about their speech. One of the group, however, wrote that if we were all the same then everyone would stutter, and what would not be so good about this would be that he would no longer be 'different' or 'special'. Only one child came up with ideas unrelated to speech.*

Think about differences in such things as looks, actions, likes and dislikes. Discuss similarities and differences in the answers that are given. Expand on some of the themes by asking questions such as: 'Why would that be difficult?...and *then* what would happen?'

8. SOMETHING IN COMMON? (P.113)

Talk about different areas of 'commonality'. For example, any other groups that the children might be members of – school groups, family groups, sports teams, etc. The aim is to help the children to look beyond physical things that they might have in common to such things as leisure interests and common aims.

9. MAKING A CHANGE (P.114)

Imagining that you have already achieved a goal can be more powerful than planning what you will have to do beforehand. Athletes are often trained to see themselves having made the perfect high jump, having achieved their personal best time, and so on. This activity sheet introduces a concept that will be used in more depth in later sections.

Talk about how things don't always turn out as we expect. I may have wished to change how I look, but then I found that when the change happened no one recognized me and I had to make friends with people all over again! Or I wished I could be faster at running so I didn't keep missing the school bus, and then I won an inter-school race!

10. THE CHANGE SHOP (P.115)

It is important to recognize parts of us that we're not happy about. This is a way of children being more accepting of who they are now so that they will be more able and ready to make changes.

Before you start this activity sheet give a few examples, such as 'I would like to sell my curly hair and exam nerves and buy a bagful of confidence for when I sing in the school play'.

Encourage elaborate descriptions of the shop and the shopkeeper. Talk about what sort of person the shopkeeper might be (e.g. very careful, friendly, sensitive) as he is going to help children to get rid of unwanted things and buy or change them for things that they really want.

Share some ideas when the activity sheets are completed. Talk about how things that some people want to sell, others might have wanted to buy. See if there is anything that can be 'exchanged' between children. For more able children you could expand on this by holding a group 'auction' of characteristics.

11. THINGS I LIKE ABOUT ME (P.116)

This activity sheet provides an opportunity to recap and bring together all the points already identified and discussed. Encourage children to include physical attributes (e.g. 'I like my hair') as well as personality attributes (e.g. 'I'm a good friend').

I have sometimes used this exercise too near the beginning of a course and have found that many children struggle to identify more than one or two things that they like about themselves. Some are unable to name even one. By leaving it until later, when they have had plenty of time to discuss the previous activity sheets, you can avoid the potential pitfall of children becoming disheartened in their struggle to complete a list of this sort.

See also GOLD activity sheets 1 and 2.

12. IMPORTANT PEOPLE (P.117)

This activity can be extended to discussing and drawing important events, places and objects. Identifying important aspects of their life helps children to develop awareness of the effect that their environment and experiences have on how they see themselves.

This could also lead on to discussions about how different people see the same things in different ways. For example, three people seeing a fight in the play-ground will all have slightly different versions of events according to their own preconceptions and perhaps their alliances with the people involved. Three people being given a piece of blank paper and a pencil but no instructions as to what to do with them will probably have very different feelings about it. For example – panic (I don't know what to do, I'm no good at deciding, I can't think up good ideas, I know that whatever I do will be wrong); enthusiasm (I can do anything that I want, I've got loads of good ideas, I love the freedom of experimenting); or anxiety expressed as anger (How am I expected to know what she wants? What does she think I am – a mindreader? She just wants to keep me quiet for a while. This is really boring).

Panic and anger are, of course, often the manifestation of low self-esteem. These three people may in the end produce three different pieces of work – one could write something, one could make a paper aeroplane and one could draw a picture. Events have a significance in themselves but, perhaps more importantly, it is the way that we interpret them that determines our consequent actions and our view of ourselves.

See also activity 13 in this section.

13. MY DISPLAY CABINET (P.118)

This activity sheet highlights the difference between 'boasting' and celebrating the things and people that we are proud of. Children can fill in the sentences and add extra ideas of their own.

Important events may not necessarily be pleasant. It might be very important to one child that she fell and broke a leg, for instance.

See notes for activity 12 in this section.

Expansion activities

(a)   Read a story to the group about differences and similarities or self-discovery.

For the younger age group I use *Something Else* by Kathryn Cave and Chris Riddell – a beautiful story about Something Else who tries to be like others but just isn't!

Another favourite is 'The House of Coloured Windows' by Margaret Mahy. This is a short story from *A Treasury of Stories for Eight Year Olds*. It tells of a girl whose greatest wish is to look through the coloured windows of a wizard's house. He tells her that she can choose the world that she likes best, but once she has chosen she must live there. Of course, from all the many different worlds she sees, she chooses to go back home.

Daisy-Head Mayzie by Dr Seuss tells of a girl who suddenly grows a daisy from the top of her head and the various reactions of the people around her to this strange 'difference'. The daisy finally disappears, but the closing pages of the book hint at its occasional return (although it seems that Mayzie is becoming accustomed to it!).

Bill's New Frock by Anne Fine explores the differences between girls and boys. A funny and thought-provoking book for all ages, this is quite lengthy and could perhaps be available for children to borrow.

Nothing by Mick Inkpen is about a toy's search to 'discover who he really is'.

(b)   Make up a story about a magic mirror.

This can be done individually, or each child in the group can add to the story in turn. If the children are willing to share their stories then I suggest that you create a special time for this at regular intervals. Cover a chair with a special cloth, dim the lights and invite each child to sit in the 'story teller's chair'. A joint story could similarly be written out and read aloud by one or two of the children.

(c)   Take turns to retell favourite fairy tales or myths from memory.

Traditional fairy tales contain a wealth of images that represent unconscious processes. They can therefore help children to understand themselves and some of the dilemmas they face.

(d)   Make and decorate a large magic mirror. Each child has a turn on different days to have her photograph or drawing displayed in the mirror.

(e)   Start a photo or self-portrait gallery of the group.

(f)   Set up a drama session where each child moves around the room as their chosen animal. As they pass they greet each other without using words. (RUBIES activity sheet 2 (p.44).)

(g)   Have a display area where each child puts one special item or photograph that is important to them.

(h)   Have a 'bring a friend day' when each child brings a photo or drawing of a friend, family member or pet and tells the group about this 'friend'.

(i)   Experiment with 'change'. For example, everyone tries sitting somewhere different for a whole session, tries out a different hairstyle (even if it's just parting their hair in a different place) or wears something of a certain colour (you will need to have a ready supply of paper flowers, arm bands, etc. for those children who might forget or who don't have anything made of the chosen colour). Talk about how easy or difficult it was to make these changes.

(j)   Play the mirror game. Children sit facing each other in pairs. They take it in turns silently and slowly to move their arms, hands, shoulders and head, while their partner tries to mirror their movements.

(k)   Spend time together researching rubies.

III

Friends and Feelings (SILVER)

Aims of this section

- to further develop the use of imagework

- to explore the social skill of asking questions

- to explore and name a variety of feelings

- to understand more about the nature of feelings and how different feelings might lead to different ways of behaving

- to explore the nature of friendships

Additional materials

- card and safety pins for making badges

- coloured card for making friendship cards

Successful friendships are a powerful influence on a child's level of self-esteem and confidence.

> *Stephanie (11) was referred for therapy because of concerns over her moderate stutter. She made excellent progress until the point where she had to move to the next stage of her schooling. Her two best friends went to a different school. Her parents had initiated an appeal but unfortunately, for*

various reasons, Stephanie had to continue at her new school for several months.

During this time her teachers tried to encourage friendships between Stephanie and some of her new classmates, but Stephanie's stutter became progressively worse and she became more and more withdrawn. She said that she had no friends and no one liked her. She began to somatize her feelings ('mistaking' an emotional ache for a physical one). She complained of stomachache and sickness. Finally, Stephanie was able to change schools to be with her friends, and within a matter of days her speech had become markedly more fluent. Her parents reported that she was 'like a different child' – confident and happy and positively enjoying school!

Activity worksheets

INTRODUCTORY PAGE (P.120)

I suggest reading this together. Introductory pages are not intended to be used as an exercise in reading competency unless you specifically want to incorporate this into a planned lesson.

Facilitate a general discussion about friendships. Aim for the children to direct comments and questions to each other rather than through you. Allowing children to participate in collaborative discussion, rather than simple question-and-answer sessions, helps them to learn more readily and to develop a firmer level of self-esteem and a better understanding of social skills. However, for this to work well you will need to have done preliminary work on group gelling and establishing group rules (see 'Working with a group', pp.31–32). It may be useful for the group to recap on these 'rules' before starting the discussion.

1. TELLING PEOPLE ABOUT MYSELF (P.121)

This exercise helps children to reflect on the activities that they did in the previous section and then moves them on to thinking more about how they interact with other people.

2. FINDING OUT A BIT MORE (P.122)

A chance to stretch the imagination again and to think about the social skill of asking questions. Talk about different types of question. Encourage open questions that would invite more detailed answers, rather than closed questions that might result in single word answers such as yes or no.

Try this out in role-play (see expansion activities).

3. FEELINGS (P.123)

See note for RUBIES activity sheet 2 (p.44).

To help children to think about this in more depth, discuss feelings of being in the group on the first day, their first day at school, first time in an after-school club, etc. Explore suggestions as to what made it OK or what might have made it easier (e.g. going with a friend, meeting the teacher beforehand, visiting the building and looking round, talking it over with a friend or adult).

4. HOW MANY FEELINGS? (P.124)

I am always surprised by how many feeling words a group of children can come up with once they get going! The more words they know, the more they will be able to express what they are feeling without having to show it non-verbally (children may somatize feelings because they don't know how to tell us what is worrying them or because they don't recognize the feeling).

It is vital to let children know that all feelings are real and valid. It is how we *express* them that is important. Anger doesn't have to lead to physical aggression. Feeling scared or shy doesn't have to lead to avoidance. Feeling excited doesn't necessarily have to involve tearing round the classroom like a wild horse!

Do a verbal round of 'I feel _____'. This exercise, especially if done regularly, encourages children to recognize their own feelings and hopefully to come to understand that other people cannot *make* us feel anything. You might want to specifically make this point. Our feelings are how we have chosen (albeit subconsciously) to react.

5. HOW I FEEL (P.125)

Children are often labelled according to their behaviour at an early age and they quickly absorb these labels into their belief system about themselves. If a child has always been told 'You're so grumpy all the time', then that is what he will believe and he is likely to act accordingly. Unfortunately it is often the case that once this belief system is established, trying to change how a child views himself by telling him the opposite (in this case, perhaps, 'You seem very happy today') rarely works effectively. He will have to experience it often enough and think enough of himself for this to have an impact.

Choose some scenarios from the completed activity sheets and discuss whether other children have been in a similar situation but felt something different.

Compare all the different things that lead to each child feeling excited or nervous.

Talk about how different people feel different things at different times. Talk about how feelings can change – what we might once have been nervous about we might eventually come to enjoy or to feel more confident about.

Point out any feelings that are similar in the group ('It sounds as though most people get excited when _____.' 'Almost everyone feels nervous when _____.').

6. IMAGINING THAT FEELINGS ARE COLOURS (P.126)

Talk about how we can feel like a different colour at different times on different days. Our moods change, and that means that uncomfortable feelings, as well as nice feelings, will change, stop or go away.

Help the children to elaborate on how they would move if they were being different colours. Invite two or more children at a time to move around the room as if they were being a certain colour. See if the rest of the group can correctly guess the colour.

Too many changes too quickly can be very difficult to cope with. Brainstorm ideas for what we can do to keep our feelings more balanced. For example, if I keep feeling angry I can:

- tell someone that I'm feeling angry

- sit and do a quiet activity until I feel more calm

- go and scribble in an 'angry book'

- write down all the things I'm angry about

- think about what I'm going to do later that I'm looking forward to

- daydream about the thing I'd like to happen that would mean I wasn't angry any more (wouldn't it be wonderful if I could have that new computer game/stay up late/go to the park – if I was invisible/a giant/an adult/I would _____!).

Of course, sometimes children don't know why they are feeling something. Acknowledging an unpleasant feeling can still help to dissipate it without the need to analyse it.

7. TEASING (P.127)

Invariably, children with low self-esteem are victims of teasing or bullying or they resort to being the teaser or bully themselves. Discussions about teasing are always lengthy in the groups I run. The intensity of focused concentration often needs to be relieved by an active game at the end.

Brainstorm different ways that people tease each other such as name-calling, taking and playing with treasured possessions, copying the way that someone walks or talks, consistently ignoring someone, and so on.

Brainstorm why people might tease – because they want to feel 'big', because they have been teased themselves, they've just been told off, they don't understand that what they are saying or doing is hurtful, etc.

8. GETTING THE PICTURE (PP.128–129)

This exercise is taken from my earlier book *Using Interactive Imagework with Children* (pp.127–128).

Read the exercise very slowly with plenty of pauses for the children to explore their images. As before, ask for verbal feedback when appropriate (see notes for EMERALDS activity sheet 1 (p.41) and RUBIES activity sheet 2 (p.44)). Invite the children to talk about their images after they have drawn them. Compare and contrast the ideas. Point out similarities and differences in the images produced. As with all images, reinforce the idea that there are no right or wrong images, they all show different ways of looking at the problem.

9. MORE ON TEASING (P.130)

When you brainstorm 'what to do' be sure to accept all the contributions, including those relating to fighting back. Once they have all been written on the chart or whiteboard, talk about the consequences of each action. What would happen if you hit them? What would happen if you told a grown up? Children have often been told to 'ignore' the person who is teasing, but I have never yet had a group where all the members agreed on this strategy. Many children tell me they've tried this 'but it doesn't work'.

Brainstorming the options and their consequences usually results in some useful ideas that children are more likely to try because they've come up with these solutions themselves.

> *In a recent group one boy suggested that he could stutter so much that he would get into the* Guinness Book of Records; *then he would become rich and famous, and the bullies would be really jealous! This led on to all sorts of other amazing ideas, but the group finally settled on a combination of telling an adult and saying something like 'I can stutter much better than you can' if anyone copied the way that they spoke. One child in the group still felt that he would risk the consequences and hit out, because that's what his dad had recommended!*

10. ALL ABOUT MY FRIEND (P.131)

Important aspects can be written around or inside the frame such as J. likes toffee, J. is ace at mending things.

11. RECIPE FOR A GOOD FRIEND (P.132)

You can choose to be quite literal about this and have a potion of things like 'good at listening', 'good at sharing', 'fun', and so on (but see activity sheet 12 in this section).

Alternatively, this is a chance to explore the imagination even more and be wild and wacky with the potion ingredients! Christopher (7), whose school had expressed concern about his imaginative abilities, put an iguana, mud, a frog and chocolate cake amongst his ingredients!

12. THE HOUSE OF FRIENDSHIP (P.133)

This activity provides children with the chance to expand their vocabulary around the theme of friendships and to begin to think about the importance and the difficulties of friendships in more depth. Brainstorm this in the group first, and leave plenty of time for the children to fill in their own sheets with the words that are most important to them. Aim for a mixture of different aspects of friendships.

13. WHAT MAKES A GOOD FRIEND? (P.134)

The aim here is to help children to think more about what a person can do to *form* friendships as well as to identify why it is that they 'get on with' a particular friend.

Discuss the variety of answers that come up and lead this on to a discussion about having friends who are different from each other. For example, two very different people might be friends with a child but not particularly close friends with each other. Encourage the children to think why that might be.

14. SPECIAL PERSON FOR THE DAY (P.135)

Make a Special Person Badge. Children can take turns at being 'special' and have special privileges. It is best to have a random method of choosing children for this, such as putting names in unmarked envelopes or inside balloons and then popping one or more balloons at each session.

We usually have at least two special people each day when we run intensive courses for children who stutter. Their treats include extra biscuits and drinks at break times, being picked first for games and having a praise card designed and written by the rest of the group with at least six different praises on it.

Adam (8) is a bouncy child with some mild language difficulties and a tense repetitive stutter. For a long time he has held the view that stuttering is his fault and that he should try harder to control it. He was accepted on a two-week course as it was felt that he would make more progress intensively than with weekly individual therapy. It was also felt that both he and his parents would benefit from meeting other children who stutter. Adam has a tendency to shout out and to jump around like a 'live wire'. Inevitably, he frequently drops things, bumps into people or says things that others find funny or irritating. He finds it extremely difficult to write legibly and tends to do everything in a rush. Adam insisted on praising everyone for 'using common sense'. This was not something we had talked about in the group at all. The therapists guessed that it might be something that he heard regularly from others.

His excitement over the possibility of being special person mounted as the days passed. On the second Monday of the course he told me that at the weekend he had slept with all his fingers crossed and was sure that today would be the day! Sure enough it was! He left the room (hugging himself!) while the rest of the group thought up praises for him. One of the older members pointed out that he might like to be praised for having common sense. This was duly written on Adam's card. When the card was completed and read out to Adam he couldn't stop grinning for the rest of the morning! I later overheard the same older boy praise Adam for being 'intelligent'.

The crowning glory was when Adam remarked to me that he not only thought he had done a particular activity sheet very sensibly and carefully but also thought it was 'probably' OK to stutter a little bit.

15. MY SPECIAL FRIENDSHIP DAY (P.136)

See note for RUBIES activity sheet 9 (p.47).

Discuss differences and similarities in people's ideas for their special day. Is there anything that could actually be incorporated into your self-esteem sessions?

16. SHARING (P.137)

Invite children to work in pairs for this one. Do a final discussion in the large group to bring together all the ideas. Focus on what makes sharing easy or hard and why sharing is important. Encourage a range of examples for things that can be shared (e.g. ideas, conversations, special moments, worries, secrets, friends, as well as perhaps more obvious things like games, sweets, toys, etc.).

17. WHEN BEING A FRIEND IS DIFFICULT (P.138)

See previous notes on 'looking back' at a situation (e.g. RUBIES activity sheet 9 (p.47)).

18. MORE THAN ONE (P.139)

See notes for EMERALDS activity sheet 1 (p.41) and RUBIES activity sheet 5 (pp.45–46).

Before doing this activity, talk about the things that we can do to help groups to go well. Invite suggestions as to how different people might feel in a group and how feelings can change from the start of a group to the end of a group. Introduce the idea of endings – that if a particular group or friendship comes to an end that means that something new will be starting. Talk about the feelings that might be associated with this.

19. THE MAGIC MIRROR (P.140)

This does not have to be a self-portrait again. Children might choose to draw a picture of two people or a group playing together or talking together. They could draw something that represents what they feel when they are with friends. Encourage children to look back over the activity sheets they have done in this section and then to be creative in whatever they want to put in the mirror.

Expansion activities

(a)   Read a story about friendships or sharing. I have used the following:

The Selfish Crocodile by Faustin Charles and Michael Terry. This is the story of a crocodile that refuses to share the river with any other animals. He develops toothache but no animal will help him because they are too scared. A mouse dares to enter the crocodile's mouth, and all is resolved in the end.

Something Else by Kathryn Cave and Chris Riddell (see p.49)

A lengthier book, but worth lending out or reading a chapter at a time as part of your planned session, is *Friends and Brothers* by Dick King-Smith.

(b)   Design an interview questionnaire together and ask each child either to interview one person in the group or to complete as a 'do at home' activity. For example, they could ask questions such as 'How old are you? What is your favourite TV programme? What do you like doing after school?' and so on.

(c)   Draw pictures to express different feelings. These can be representative, such as a smiley face, or symbolic, such as a firework for excitement. Rachel (9) drew me pictures of how she felt when her talking was easy and how she felt when it was difficult. Her easy picture showed her sitting in an armchair on a high platform overlooking a green field. She gave it the title 'enjoyable'. Her difficult speaking picture consisted of a red scribble with purple zigzags exploding from it. She called this one 'angry'. Her anger and frustration, clearly evident in the way she tackles her speech difficulty, were forcefully and very successfully expressed in this second picture.

(d)   Make cards for friends.

(e)   Make up a co-operative poem or short story about friendships. Each person contributes one word or one sentence in turn. This works well if an adult acts as scribe and reads the composition to the group when it is completed.

(f)   Set up role-play situations – meeting someone for the first time; sorting out a friendly argument; dealing with teasing.

(g)   Write out several different feeling words on separate cards and several different activities (e.g. washing up, writing a letter). Children take it in turns to pick one card from each group and mime the combination (e.g. washing up angrily). The rest of the group try to guess what is happening.

(h)   Play 'team machine'. Small groups of children think of a machine that involves several working parts. They then work out a co-operative mime for the rest of the children to guess what machine they are being.

IV

Feeling OK about Being Me (GOLD)

Aims of this section

- to identify current strengths
- to begin to think about areas for further work
- to introduce the idea of skill building
- to identify some of the elements that constitute a feeling of confidence
- to introduce the idea of accepting praise

Additional materials

- softball or beanbag for the circle game

Activity worksheets

INTRODUCTORY PAGE (P.142)

See previous notes on using introductory pages.

Encourage each child to say how he is feeling today.

1. PRIZE-GIVING DAY (P.143)

Many adults have told me that they would find this task very difficult! Most children, however, will come up with plenty of ideas once they have been given a few pointers; such as: What about an award for making friends? Mending things? Playing football? Singing?

> *Marcus (12) was one of the children who could not think of anything at all to write in his star. He screwed up the activity sheet and threw it away. No amount of coaxing could persuade him to write anything on a new sheet. We eventually decided that every time he discovered something he would like an award for he could go back and add it to the star. This was a long process for him, but he did eventually find ten things. Occasionally he would ask me to confirm a thought – 'Do you think I'm any good at making friends?' – and we would try and think of concrete examples that showed that he was indeed 'good' at this.*

I would like to add a note here about the use of the word 'good'. I believe that it should be used sparingly since it carries such a weighty opposite in most children's minds – if I am not good at something then I must be bad. The reason for the 'good' should be explained whenever possible. 'Good boy' is not really specific enough (I'm obviously being good but I'm not sure exactly what I've done). 'That's a good piece of work' is non-specific and potentially judgemental – what then is a 'bad' piece of work? Am I at risk of being bad or doing a bad piece of work without realizing it? This is particularly relevant, of course, when a child has created something – remarks such as 'that's a good picture' or 'that's a good construction' or a 'good poem' are personal opinions rather than de-scriptions.

I try to encourage parents to avoid talking about periods of stuttering in terms such as 'he was really bad yesterday' but to think of it as something like 'it was a difficult day for him yesterday'. There are plenty of alternatives to 'good' and 'bad' that can be used instead. We cannot afford to underestimate the power of words and their contribution to a child's perceptions of himself (see also notes for STARS activity sheets (pp.37–40)).

Having discussed this at length with a student speech and language therapist I nevertheless found myself overusing 'good' in the very next therapy session she observed. Changing habits takes time!

2. LOADS OF AWARDS (P.144)

It is important to spend time talking about achievements with others. Having a list is not usually enough to validate them fully.

Each child could choose one of their achievements to tell to the group or in pairs.

Talk about the different things that people like to get as awards. Many children will write that they got a new computer game or something else hugely expensive but in reality most are also very proud to receive certificates, medals, and so on.

As youngsters we rely heavily on external praise and rewards to help us to build self-esteem and a strong sense of who we are. It is not long, however, before we have to learn to internalize our praise. In other words, to recognize our own achievements and praise ourselves. Encouraging children to look at things that they feel positive about is part of this process. For example, you can feel positive about your ability to run fast even without winning a medal for this!

3. THINGS I'M WORKING ON (P.145)

Children often think of these as 'things I can't do' or 'things I'm no good at'. Whenever appropriate, if you hear them using these phrases you might suggest that they feel what it's like to change the words to 'I'm working on ____'. If it's something that they are NOT working on because it simply isn't important to them (I personally don't need to learn how to change a car tyre because I no longer have a car), then rather than 'I'm no good at this' they could try 'I don't need to learn/practise this'. Watch out for the child who then uses this as an excuse for not working on anything!

Talk about how it is OK to make mistakes when we are learning things. When we make mistakes we find out how *not* to do things. This can sometimes help us to be more inventive in finding out successful ways to achieve our goals.

4. MORE AWARDS (P.146)

See notes for activity sheets 2 and 3 in this section.

Emphasize that these awards are for all the effort that is needed when we are working on something that we find difficult.

Talk about all the different feelings that could be associated with being rewarded.

5. STAR TURN (P.147)

Initiate a round of 'I'm brilliant at _____' in the group. Discuss the variety of things that come up. If you feel it's appropriate you could talk about how people get to be brilliant at something. For example, this might involve discussion on learning 'sets' of skills and building up ability gradually. This can be compared to having a natural ability at something that might nevertheless need to be practised and developed (such as singing).

6. CONFIDENCE (P.148)

Confidence is quite a nebulous concept, especially for children. What is it? How do we get it? Big questions! One way of thinking about this is to decide on a person that the children all agree *appears* very confident. This might be a TV personality or a fictional character or someone they all know. Make a list together of all the things that this person does that causes them to appear confident. Be as specific as possible. If someone says 'they *look* confident', then talk about how the person stands, walks, sits, dresses, etc. If they say 'they *sound* confident', talk about *how* they sound – Fast? Slow? Loud? Soft? Somewhere in between?

The process of having identified some concrete things to do and ways to act will go some way towards helping children to *create* a feeling of confidence when needed.

7. LET'S IMAGINE (P.149)

This exercise uses imagework to explore confidence in more depth and to help children to begin to experience it in actuality, rather than just talking about it. See previous notes on imagework exercises (e.g. EMERALDS activity sheet 1 (p.41) and RUBIES activity sheet 5 (pp.45–46)).

Encourage discussion around the images that the children produced. For example, talk about the way that they imagined their CONFIDENT moved and felt. Relate this to how we can act in a confident way. Discuss the different points that children came up with relating to the positive things about being a CONFIDENT, also anything that they thought of that was not so helpful.

8. I FELT CONFIDENT (P.150)

Relate this exercise to previous discussions about feeling different things at different times. See SILVER activity sheets 3, 4, 5 and 6.

9. PRAISE (P.151)

See previous notes on praise, particularly the note on STARS activity sheet 3 (pp.38–39) and for activity sheets 1 and 2 in this section.

> *Paul (10) is a tall lad for his age and complains that he is often thought of as being older than he really is. He is expected to act in a 'grown-up' way and it seems that to a certain degree this includes being 'manly' in coping with emotions as well. When taking part in a praise circle in a group with ten other boys he showed us the qualities and characteristics that he perhaps really valued or wanted for himself when he praised others for being 'as gentle as a butterfly' and 'light and small'.*

10. THE MAGIC MIRROR (P.152)

As before, a chance to recap and decide on one aspect of this section to record with a drawing.

Expansion activities

(a)   Read a story about confidence. There are plenty of children's books about confidence and feeling OK about yourself. These are some that I have used:

Scaredy Cat by Anne Fine. Poppy is afraid of ghosts and monsters but needs to find a way of showing her classmates that she is not a 'scaredy-cat'.

Only a Show by Anne Fine. Anna is worried about doing a five-minute show for her class. She is worried that she isn't confident, clever or funny and that she can't do anything 'special'. In the end, her show is a triumph.

I'm Scared by Bel Money. A book exploring some of the things that young children are often afraid of. Kitty is afraid of the dark but she is able to come to the rescue when other children are afraid of things.

Fergus the Forgetful by Margaret Ryan and Wendy Smith. Fergus can never remember things like taking his PE kit or his homework to school, but he is a mine of information about 'important' things and manages to help his school win a quiz.

(b)   Display pictures of 'things I'm brilliant at'. See if children can guess the owner of each picture.

(c)   Each child chooses a special word to describe herself, beginning with the first letter of her name (e.g. Energetic Erin, Smiley Sally). Stand in a circle and use a softball or beanbag to throw. On the first round the catcher says her own special name. On the second round the thrower calls out another child's special name as she throws the ball/beanbag to her.

(d)   Make lists of 'things I've learnt today' (not necessarily things learnt in the group).

(e)   Display the CONFIDENT pictures. Talk about the opposite of being confident. Draw pictures to represent this opposite.

(f)   Make collaborative pictures to show ways of praising or to show achievements. Join several large sheets of paper so that groups of children can sit round in a circle or square to add their bit. This is a good exercise in co-operation and in trying to see things from another person's perspective. They will need to decide which way up the picture is going to be, how best to divide up the space, whether they will allow any overlap of pictures, and so on. For older children, this can form a good basis for discussion on maintaining group co-operation.

V

Taking Care
of Myself (PEARLS)

Aims of this section

- to help children to identify their own self-help resources

- to introduce the idea of needing to prepare for difficult challenges

- to help children to be aware of the physical feelings associated with anxiety and how they can have some control over these

- to encourage self-monitoring of feelings and thoughts

- to encourage identification of worries and concerns and to show children that they can develop successful ways of dealing with these

Additional materials

- a box to decorate and post worries into (activity sheet 12)

Activity worksheets

INTRODUCTORY PAGE (P.154)

Compare and contrast 'taking care' while doing something (such as school work) and looking after ourselves.

Take time for a brief recap of the treasure that has already been collected.

1. PREPARE TO DIVE! (P.155)

I originally had the symbol of going mountain climbing for this activity sheet but eventually decided that I have personally done a fair bit of that (metaphorically, not literally!) and would rather use a symbol of diving. The idea of finding pearls, albeit amongst wrecks and seaweed, really appeals to me!

This exercise can be used as a starting point for discussion on the importance of preparing for new or difficult things.

2. FEELINGS (P.156)

The interaction between mind and body has been studied extensively and much has been written about it, especially in recent years. You will find a brief summary in *Using Interactive Imagework with Children*. The main points are:

- The mind and the body are in constant communication with each other as different 'systems' of the body respond to messages from the mind and vice versa. For example, research using biofeedback systems has shown that children who suffer from migraines can significantly affect their ability to control these by using relaxation imagery. What they *think* can affect their body.

- The imagination also directly affects the autonomic nervous system (ANS) – the part of our nervous system that controls such things as heart rate, breathing, circulation, body temperature and digestive processes.

- Worrying about (or getting excited about) an event long before it happens can cause the body to react as though the event were actually happening now.

3. FEELING TENSE (P.157)

See previous notes on imagework (e.g. EMERALDS activity sheet 1 (p.41) and RUBIES activity sheet 2 (p.44)).

By exploring some feelings in more depth we are helping children to begin to take responsibility for their feelings – a skill of value throughout life.

4. FEELING RELAXED (P.158)

I usually use this activity sheet after actually doing a relaxation with the children. Learning to relax the mind and body is a skill that needs to be practised regularly in order to reap its long-term benefits. Even the most tense-looking children can eventually learn to let go of unnecessary muscle tension during relaxation sessions.

I tend not to use the progressive relaxation methods very often (tensing then relaxing different muscle groups) as I find that some children tense up so much they find it hard to let go again! Mostly I use a method of focusing on different parts of the body and letting relaxation happen at its own pace (see Appendix E). Sometimes I use music or story telling to facilitate this.

You may have your own favourite method of relaxation to use, but it is worth experimenting with different types over a few sessions and asking for feedback from the children as to which one they found most helpful.

If any children want to (they usually do!) then take time to share the imagework pictures of being tense and being relaxed.

> *Laura (10), who at first told me she couldn't draw, produced a picture of herself lying on a sun lounger beneath a palm tree. Matthew (9) drew his cat curled up in front of the fire at home. Simon (9) drew a sunset. All very different. All expressing the feeling of relaxation.*

5. BECOMING THE IMAGE (P.159)

See previous notes on imagework.

Ways of relaxing can most easily be learnt in childhood. It is much more difficult, though not impossible, to alter stress patterns in adulthood.

Talk about the different physical sensations that we produce in our body when we are relaxed.

6. GROWING HAPPY FEELINGS (P.160)

Discuss the different ideas that people come up with. Celebrate the differences!

7. RELAXED BREATHING (P.161)

Take some time to look at pictures of the lungs and trachea (windpipe). This may seem a bit technical after the imagework sessions. However, I believe that it is useful to demystify the workings of the body so that children can realize that they have the ability to change their automatic reactions to stress and anxiety when these are not helpful to them.

The missing words are:

lungs

oxygen

in

out

out

lungs

in

lungs

8A. AND 8B. AN IMAGE FOR CALM BREATHING (PP.162–163)

See previous notes on imagework (e.g. EMERALDS activity sheet 1 (p.41) and RUBIES activity sheet 2 (p.44)).

9. TAKING CARE OF MYSELF EVERY DAY (P.164)

Contrast different ways that people (children *and* adults) choose to relax. Highlight the need to unwind in some way when things have been very busy. Talk about mental and emotional 'busyness' as well as physical 'busyness'.

10. HOW TO MAKE A PERFECT DAY (P.165)

Encourage fantastical answers again. Giving children their wishes in fantasy can be a great way of relieving pent-up frustration (see notes for SILVER activity sheet 6 (pp.55–56))

11. LETTING GO OF WORRIES (P.166)

Sometimes, if worries can't be dealt with straightaway, they do at least need to be deposited or off-loaded somewhere. The HugMe tree is designed to be just such a place (but it needs a hug afterwards!).

12. ANY MORE WORRIES? (P.167)

Facilitate a discussion about what could happen to the worries. Encourage fantasy solutions as well as more practical ones. For example: They should be tied up in a bundle and sent to _____ who would read each one and discuss them with _____. Laws would be passed to make _____ illegal. Everyone who had ever worried about _____ would receive _____. All the worries would then be _____.

The worry box is always well used in our therapy groups. Because the worries will be read out it is, of course, important to tell the children beforehand that the worries will be brainstormed in the group (they are posted anonymously). I know that some schools use this idea. They may well have some worries posted that would need to be taken further because they potentially involve others. In our groups, worries tend to centre quite naturally on speech and language difficulties and feelings of anxiety when speaking. There was once a worry about nightmares posted and the group came up with some excellent suggestions for dealing with this. Once the worry has been discussed it is ceremoniously torn up or put through the shredder.

Craig (7) was having a tough time at school because he was finding 'everything too hard'. He began to cry every morning and to plead with his mother to keep him at home. Craig and I wrote an 'I hate school because' list outlining all his worries. We made two versions — one for him to talk about with his mother and one to go in the worry box — with each worry on a separate slip of paper. In fact, unasked, Craig re-wrote his list at home and decorated it. His mother took it to school and discussed the contents with the head teacher. Within days the worries had been mostly addressed and Craig had stopped crying in the mornings. On his next visit to see me he asked if we could tear up all the worries except one that hadn't been 'fixed' yet!

13. THE WORRY TEAM (P.168)

Facilitate a discussion about what could happen to worries. Ask questions such as: 'What would you like your worries to do? Imagine this happening. What happens next? Then what happens?'

For example, worries can disappear, grow bigger, shrink or change into something else.

14. THE MAGIC MIRROR (P.169)

See previous notes on using the magic mirror (pp.44 and 60).

Expansion activities

(a)   Read a story about worries or a story about a perfect day.

My books about worries became well worn very quickly! I like the classic Dr Seuss book *I Had Trouble in Getting to Solla Sollew* – a 'fable' about facing up to your troubles. Also popular amongst the children (and, I have to say, amongst many of my colleagues!) is *The Huge Bag of Worries* by Virginia Ironside. Wonderfully illustrated by Frank Rodgers, this is the story of a young girl whose bag of worries gets bigger and bigger and no one seems to be able to help until the old lady from next door suggests something radical – open it up and show the worries some daylight!

I have also used *I'm Worried* by Brian Moses, one of the 'Your Feelings' series. This contains notes for parents and teachers with lots of suggestions for group activities and discussions. Further reading books are listed at the end, and the author writes that the activities will 'satisfy a number of attainment targets in the National Curriculum Guidelines for English at Key Stage 1'.

(b)   Outline different situations and talk about what children might specifically do, using ideas from all the activity sheets completed.

I usually suggest that children come up with at least three things that they can do for each situation. For example:

When x happens I will _____

When I notice myself getting uptight/feeling cross I will _____

When I feel happy I will _____

(c)   Take turns to say something nice that's happened today even if it's 'I had a tasty breakfast'.

(d)   Make a worry box and problem-solve any worries that find their way into it.

(e)   Do a relaxation session and tape it so that individual children can use this on a regular basis. See Appendix E for a suggested relaxation script.

(f)   Make a giant paper HugMe tree to put on the wall. This can be used to hang up worries or 'things I'm proud of'.

(g)   Make up group or individual stories about worries, e.g. 'The Day the Worries Took Over Our School!'

VI

More Than Just Talking (SAPPHIRES)

Aims of this section

- to identify the various elements that contribute to successful communication

- to help children to identify their own strengths and areas to work on with regard to communication

- to explore the variety of ways in which we express ourselves

Additional materials

No additional materials are required for this section.

Activity worksheets

INTRODUCTORY PAGE (P.171)

This could be used in a speech and language therapy group to promote discussion about various things that can happen to someone's speech. Even in a non-therapy group I feel that it is important for children to discuss this, though perhaps not in as much depth. It heightens awareness of natural differences and also of the fact that many people get anxious about speaking at times, whether or not they have a specific speech difficulty.

1. ALL ABOUT HOW WE TALK (P.172)

Speech and language therapists may want to discuss this in depth. Again, it is useful for any group to explore how we speak in order to help children to be more tolerant of differences, and also more tolerant of their own natural mistakes.

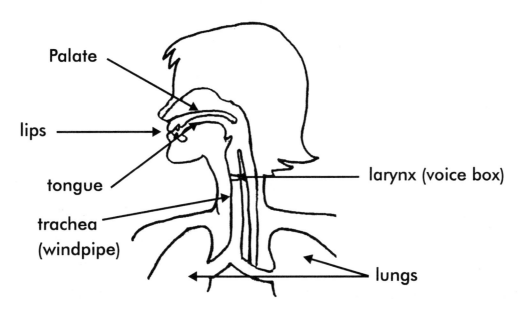

2. CONVERSATIONS (P.173)

An activity sheet to encourage children to think about wider issues other than just speech.

Talk about the wide variety of different types of conversation – with one other person, in groups, about something serious, during play, about something familiar, about something new, and so on.

3. TALKING SKILLS (P.174)

Children might just give quick, unconsidered answers to the four specific questions on this activity sheet. To encourage a much wider range of ideas, brainstorm in the large group if you feel it is necessary.

4. LISTENING SKILLS (P.175)

An activity sheet to encourage children to think about listening as a skill which requires some focusing of attention. Talk about how we can sometimes hear several things at the same time (e.g. the television, someone talking and the phone ringing), but we can choose which one to actually listen to.

5A. LET'S IMAGINE (PP.176–177)

There are several possible areas for discussion arising from this activity sheet. Use a role-play situation engineered between two adults if you think your group would pick out the important social skills, or lack of them, by watching and listening rather than from a story.

5B. MIKE AND BILL (P.178)

Discuss the alternative, more successful scenario, demonstrating social skills if needed.

6. TAKING TURNS (P.179)

Relate your discussion to a variety of activities that require turn-taking if they are to work well. For example: team games; a joint story telling; board games; as well as conversations. Demonstrate a conversation with another adult where turn-taking is not used and compare this to a conversation where you both take more or less equal turns. Encourage children to role-play this in small groups.

This activity sheet can be used to give children with a speech difficulty the chance to say how they feel when others don't give them time to talk.

7. LOOKING (P.180)

You will need to be aware of any cultural issues related to this. For example, it may not be appropriate for some children to use prolonged eye contact with certain adults.

8. KEEPING GOOD EYE CONTACT (P.181)

Ideas might include: walking slowly around the room and greeting as many people as possible by gaining eye contact with them and smiling; talking for one minute on a chosen topic whilst trying to look at everyone in the group at least once; watching a video or TV programmes and observing the level of eye contact for different speakers and listeners.

9. BODY TALK (P.186)

Act out different emotions and see if the children can guess how you are feeling. Talk about both obvious body language and more subtle things like looking away.

10. HOW DO WE SOUND WHEN WE TALK? (P.183)

This exercise helps to highlight differences and similarities in how people talk. For therapy with children who have particular speech difficulties it could lead on to more specific discussion about what can go wrong with speech.

11. SPEAKING IN A GROUP (P.184)

Compare and contrast groups of various sizes and who might be in each group. Do different children have different perspectives about groups?

Discuss what can be done to help the person who is talking (listen, sit still, keep good eye contact, smile, ask questions, etc.).

12. WHAT I FEEL ABOUT SPEAKING IN A GROUP (P.185)

Talk about what helps and what hinders. Help the children to problem-solve wherever possible.

13. WHAT I LIKE ABOUT THE WAY I TALK (P.186)

An exercise in recapping on the section and formulating a clear picture of successful communication skills. For example: I listened; I took turns; I asked questions; and so on. This is the list of dos and don'ts that one group of 9–11 year olds came up with when asked to produce an information video about talking skills:

- Don't change the subject.
- Don't be distracted.
- Keep good eye contact.
- Take turns; don't interrupt.
- Don't rush.
- Keep the right distance away. Not too close and not too far away from the other person.
- Talk loud enough.
- Listen carefully.
- Don't be boring.
- Ask the other person questions.

- Don't talk about something the other person is not interested in.
- Add to the conversation; make comments.
- Don't think about yourself all the time.
- Encourage the other person.

14. THE MAGIC MIRROR (P.187)

This could be an image to represent a successful conversation. (The image that just came into my mind was the keyboard used to communicate with the aliens in *Close Encounters of the Third Kind*.)

Expansion activities

(a)   Invite the children to move around the room greeting each other silently. Discuss different ways of starting and ending a conversation both verbally and silently.

(b)   Have whole conversations with no words. This is an enjoyable way to explore body language.

(c)   Each person try a silent conversation between their left and right hand – an argument, a friendly discussion about what to do on Saturday, or one being happy and the other sad. Children to then work in pairs to see if they can add spoken dialogue to each other's 'plays'. Volunteers to show both versions to the group.

(d)   Take turns to give two-minute talks on any topic of the child's choice.

(e)   Watch part of a popular TV soap opera and pick out different examples of body language.

(f)   Problem-solve how to join a conversation as a late arrival to a group.

(g)   Play Chinese whispers and talk about listening skills.

VII

Solving Problems (RAINBOWS)

Aims of this section

- to help children to see that there are lots of different ways of solving problems

- to explore the idea that not all problems are big ones

- to help children to identify the problem-solving skills that they already have

Additional materials

No additional materials are required for this section.

Activity worksheets

INTRODUCTORY PAGE (P.189)

See previous notes for introductory pages.

1. LET'S IMAGINE (P.190)

Problems are different from worries (see earlier sections). Problems are tasks, dilemmas or puzzles that are seen as being difficult and therefore need to be solved.

Greg (aged 7) drew tigers to represent some of his problems to be solved. He decided that once they'd been sorted these problems would 'pop' and disappear.

Brainstorm what to do for some common problems, e.g. you forget to take your lunch to school, your pet hamster gets out of its cage, you accidentally break something in school, someone borrows your pencils and won't give them back.

2A. A PROBLEM SHARED (P.191)

This exercise enables children to explore problems of their choice and perhaps put them more into perspective. Sometimes simply naming a problem and taking a good look at it can make it seem a lot less of a problem at all.

I have used all the activity sheets in this section with 'stutter' substituted for the word 'problem' in order to help children to explore their stuttered speech and the opposite of stuttering. 'Solving' a stutter appeals to a lot of children and they are very inventive in the images they use to depict stuttering and 'not stuttering' or 'relaxed talking', 'smooth speech' or whatever their opposite is. I recommend that only speech and language therapists try this in relation to stuttering, as you will need to know how to apply the children's images to actually helping them to maintain changes in their speech.

David (aged 10) was referred with a severe, tense stutter. He had attended several periods of therapy before we started to use imagery. David saw his stutter as a lion. It was, he told me, 'extremely big with a fluffy mane around its neck and a tail with a little bobble on the end'. Every time anyone went near the lion it roared and growled. When David became the lion and I asked him how he felt he said 'smug, happy and strong'. He said that the best thing about being this lion was that 'basically I can intimidate just about everything'. The worst thing, however, was that 'no one wants to be around me'. I asked the lion if he could see David standing nearby and if so, what did he look like? The lion said that David looked 'absolutely terrified'. He wanted to tell David to go away, but all he could do was roar and David just stood there. We spent some time swapping between David and the lion. David asked the lion to be friendly and to purr instead of roar. The lion was surprised that anyone would want to make friends with it! It could not promise only to purr but said that it would try to remember. David had no wish to change the lion in any other way. He acknowledged that it was there and still a lion.

David and I have done several imagery sessions together and very little actual speech control work. His stutter has become progressively less tense, and he now has several weeks at a time when it has virtually disappeared.

2B. PROBLEM TALK (P.192)

See previous activity sheet 'A problem shared'.

2C. WHERE HAS IT GONE? (P.193)

See previous two activity sheets.

2D. SOMETHING CHANGES (P.194)

Solutions are often not the opposite of the problem, nor are they halfway in between. More usually, they require elements of both ends of the spectrum, producing something new – an inspirational idea!

2E. MAKING IT HAPPEN (P.195)

It is important to concretize the images – to identify what steps could actually be taken to initiate the desired change. Even the act of identifying the steps can start the process going at some level.

3. ONE LESS PROBLEM (P.196)

Encourage recognition of previous experiences of problem-solving. Children need to recognize that they are creating new possibilities for themselves all the time.

4. STILL PUZZLED? (P.197)

This activity sheet has been added at this point because so many children are afraid to ask when they need help. They will use other strategies, such as watching other children and following their lead, or will perhaps wait passively until someone offers help. Feeling that it is OK to ask someone to repeat an instruction or to say 'I don't understand' is a big step for many children with low self-esteem. They will frequently equate it with further evidence that they are failing. Brainstorming this in a very 'matter of fact' way can help them to feel that it is a natural part of the learning process rather than a failure. Possible strategies might include:

- Ask someone to explain it to me.

- Brainstorm it with other people in the group.

- Break the instruction down into smaller bits and do one bit at a time.

- Ask for a repetition of the instruction/question.

5. A BIT OF MAGICAL WISDOM (P.198)

I'm sure that most of us have had the experience of coming up with a solution to a difficult problem when we are least expecting it. We think about it for hours and come to no conclusions; so we give up and go for a walk, and suddenly the answer seems crystal clear! Or perhaps you have tried to think of a name or a song title but couldn't remember it, then suddenly there it is just as you are falling asleep that night. Once again, naming the problem or defining the question can help to take some of the worry out of it. Inevitably the child's innate wisdom will help them to sort it, even if that wisdom tells them to ask someone for help.

6. THE MAGIC MIRROR (P.199)

See previous notes on using the magic mirror (pp.45 and 61).

Expansion activities

(a)   Read a story about solving problems. For young children you might like to use one of the following:

The Lighthouse Keeper's Lunch by Ronda and David Armitage – a tale about how to foil hungry seagulls so that the lighthouse keeper gets his lunch.

Horton Hatches the Egg by Dr Seuss. Horton is an elephant with a mission – to hatch the egg that a lazy bird has abandoned. He perseveres through all sorts of trials, including being teased by his friends, but he is triumphant in the end.

I Had Trouble in Getting to Solla Sollew by Dr Seuss (also suggested for Section V 'Taking Care of Myself').

VIII

Setting Goals (MOONBEAMS)

Aims of this section

- to introduce children to the idea of setting regular goals

- to expand on previous activities involving understanding the nature of change

- to provide a variety of ways in which children can monitor their own progress

Additional materials

No additional materials are required for this section.

Activity worksheets

INTRODUCTORY PAGE (P.201)

Talk about the sorts of targets or goals that people can set for themselves at school, with friends, in sport, in Scouts or Guides, etc.

Talk about individual targets and also group aims or goals.

1A. TAKING OFF (P.202) AND 1B. JUST THE RIGHT STAR (P.203)

There is a longer version of this exercise in *Using Interactive Imagework with Children* and it is adapted from an original exercise by Dina Glouberman

(Glouberman 1992, p.187). Projecting yourself into the future to imagine how things will turn out is a powerful aid to making changes. Such imagery requires the suspending of judgement and reality in order to act 'as if' you had already achieved some desired outcome.

It is sometimes the case that adults encourage a child to try out new things that unfortunately then result in failure because the child has no motivation to change or no concept of how achieving the goal might affect how he feels about himself. Imagery can provide a child with an opportunity to project himself forward in time in his imagination and see a positive outcome, experiencing it in his conscious mind and, in effect, creating a memory of the event as if it had already happened. This forward projection allows the child to recognize where he is at the moment – how far along the road he has already come – and to discover some of the things that he will need to know to achieve his goal. Perhaps other people will need to be involved, and the child can visualize how this might come about. He can also explore some of the things that might hold him back, things that he will have to overcome to achieve his goal.

It is important to help the children to identify particular goals before you start this exercise. I suggest that you then read these two pages to the group and ask for feedback as for the other imagery exercises.

2. A LETTER TO MYSELF (P.204)

Once again, committing the thoughts to paper makes them more real. Dina Glouberman suggests sealing up the letter and sending it to the writer at a later date – a way of reminding them where they're headed.

3. FOOTSTEPS (P.205)

The ability to set realistic and yet challenging goals is an important but often undervalued skill.

A child who sets herself goals and is ready and able to evaluate her own progress on an ongoing basis will find that she has a clearer sense of direction and purpose and can accomplish more in a short period. A sense of control leads to higher self-esteem, which is more likely to result in higher achievements.

Many children do not set themselves goals because they have had past experience of failure, or because they have heard too often that they will not be able to achieve them. The idea that this is now true ('I never manage to do what I really want') becomes their own self-limiting belief. Children usually need help to set realistic goals without being overly ambitious. We can encourage them to be clear about what they are aiming for and to recognize the benefits of achieving the goal by looking at the smaller steps that they need to take along the way.

4. IF I WERE FAMOUS (P.206)

This is another way of identifying long-term goals. It could be done as a newspaper article: think up the headline first and then fill in the details being as descriptive and precise as possible.

5. RECIPE FOR SUCCESS (P.207)

This is best done as a brainstorm first and then children can pick out individual ideas that they think would be right for them. See Chapter 5 on transfer and maintenance of skills in Part I for some basic ideas.

6. MY TREASURE CHEST (P.208)

Talk about the different treasure that the children choose. Make regular times when children can 'find' something in their treasure chest to share with the group.

7. GOAL RECORD SHEET (P.209)

The ability to evaluate your own progress is a skill which children with low self-esteem can often not manage in an objective way. They will need to try several different methods and talk over their goal record sheets with an adult and with each other so that they get used to setting their own goals and knowing how to move on to the next step.

Facilitate a discussion about 'change'. In particular, encourage children to think about the following:

- Why would someone change? For example:

    Because they want to feel better.

Because someone else suggests it.

Because they think they should.

Because they want to be like their friends.

- What do we need to have or to know in order to change? For example:

    We need to know what the change will involve.

    We may need help from others.

    We need to really want the change to work for us.

- What makes change easy or difficult? For example:

    There are lots of people making the same change.

    We have already made a similar change so we can guess what it is going to be like.

- What can we do to keep the change going? For example:

    Reward ourselves.

    Continue to set small goals.

These are just a few ideas to get things started. See also the expansion activities for Who Am I? (RUBIES) (pp.49–50).

8. I CAN CHANGE THE WAY THAT I FEEL (P.210)

Help the children to identify a 'toolkit' of things that they are going to do to keep up their confidence (or whatever their main goal is). They can then use this sheet to check off each achievement. The aim is also to help children to see that the skills and qualities they already have from other areas of life (such as perseverance and practice) can be put to good use when they are setting their goals. As each child has been working through the various activity sheets, he will, hopefully, have identified the things that will be most helpful. A possible list might be:

- I will reward myself when I have done well.

- I will take care of myself by doing something relaxing every day.

- I will answer at least one question in class every day.

- I will learn to swim.

- I will learn one new word every day.

- I will tell my teacher if I don't understand something.

- I will talk to my mum about my worries.

- I will make one new friend this term.

9. THE MAGIC MIRROR (P.211)

See previous notes on using the magic mirror (pp.45 and 60).

Expansion activities

(a) If your group is coming to an end at this point it is important to prepare the children for this and have a final award ceremony of some sort.

(b) Celebrate the completion of the activities book. Perhaps arrange a party and invite others to come and view the books and to ask the children questions.

(c) Put on an end of course play, involving all the children.

(d) Jointly make a large cake with the word 'confidence' on it and share it in the group so that everyone has a 'slice of confidence'.

See also Chapter 5 'Transfer and Maintenance of Skills'.

Part 3

Activity Worksheets

THIS BOOK BELONGS TO

Address:

Birthday:

I
STARS and EMERALDS

Getting Started

1. What are images?

Have you ever made up a story in your head? Imagined that you saw something that wasn't really there? Heard a noise and imagined it was something scary? Have you ever remembered the taste or feel of something that isn't actually in front of you? Do you ever imagine that you are somewhere else? Doing something different?

These are all images and they come from your imagination.

We all have the power of imagination and we can all use our imagination to help ourselves to sort out problems, feel good, cope with troubles when they come along and to help us to do the things we want to do.

The rest of this book is full of ways for you to use your imagination in a helpful way.

2. Finding some magic

As you do all the activities in this book it will be like learning to be a magician. You will learn about the magic of your mind and you will learn a lot about yourself and about other people too.

Everyone has a little bit of magic treasure in them but sometimes we let it lie hidden or we forget that it's there. The activities you will do with your group leader or teacher will help you to find your own magic treasure. Maybe it's that part of you that feels confident and relaxed or that part of you that can learn more easily or make good friends or overcome a difficulty or cope well with something that can't be changed.

Each part of the book has been given the name of something you could find in a magician's treasure chest so you will know when you have finished one bit and are ready to move on. The first bit of treasure for you to collect is a handful of STARS.

3. My personal record of achievements

What does the word 'achievement' mean?

Use these stars to keep a record of all your achievements while you are working through this book. Can you think of one thing that you have achieved just a little while ago to write in the first star?

4. Things I would like to achieve

_____

_____

_____

_____

_____

_____

_____

**Now let's collect
some more treasure!**

EMERALDS

1. Imagining

Let's check out what your imagination is like today. Ask someone to read the exercise 'Think of a Chocolate Cake' to you. While you are listening, imagine that you can see, hear, feel, taste and smell all the things that the person tells you about.

THINK OF A CHOCOLATE CAKE

Sit comfortably and close your eyes. Imagine that you are at home in the kitchen. Imagine that it is your birthday and someone has made you a huge great chocolate cake. It is in the fridge. You are allowed to go and get it.

Imagine yourself opening the fridge door. You see the cake on a big plate. What does it look like? You take it out of the fridge. What does the plate feel like? How do you carry the cake? What can you smell? You put the plate with the cake on it onto a table. Someone comes and cuts a big slice for you. What does this person say while they are cutting the cake?

What happens to the cake as this person starts to cut it? You reach out to take the piece of cake. What does it feel like when you touch it? Then you take a big bite. What can you taste? Can you smell anything? What do you imagine yourself saying? Now let the images fade and, when you're ready, open your eyes.

See how good you are at imagining things!

2. Talking cats

Just imagine!

Imagine that you have a pet cat that can talk. This cat would like to know all the things that you do on school days. Make a list of everything that you have to remember to do. Start your list with 'I wake up'.

1 _____

2 _____

3 _____

4 _____

5 _____

6 _____

7 _____

8 _____

9 _____

You didn't have to wait until you had done each thing again before you wrote it did you? You just *imagined* what you do each day.

3a. Becoming a cat

Let's imagine

Time to stretch your imagination a bit further. Imagine that you are a cat… Imagine that you can talk. You want to tell humans what it's like to be a cat. Here are some words you could use when you tell us. I'm sure you can think of a lot more.

Describing words (adjectives):

warm   furry   soft   happy   sleepy   tired

Doing words (verbs):

purr   stretch   jump   climb   run   chase   stroke

eat   drink

Naming words (nouns):

friend   basket   fish   milk

Close your eyes so that you can really begin to str-e-tch your imagination. Imagine yourself being a cat… Imagine what that feels like.

Ask someone to write down what you say while you are imagining that you are a cat. Think of a good cat name and then start with that.

3b Being a cat

My name is _____

_____

_____

_____

_____

_____

_____

_____

Imagine that!

II
RUBIES

Who Am I?

Well done – three emeralds collected so far and you've started to str-e-tch your imagination! Now you are going to collect a bagful of magic rubies while you find out a little more about being you!

Let's imagine that you have a magic mirror. Whenever you look into the mirror it will show you how you are getting along with collecting your magic treasure and learning about yourself and other people. Start by drawing yourself as you are now or, if you like, you could paste on a photograph of yourself.

1. The magic mirror

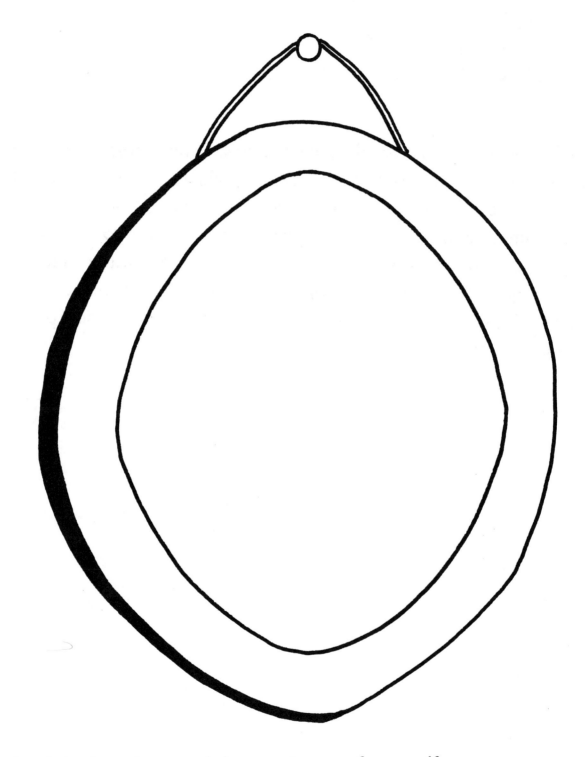

Look in the mirror and draw a picture of yourself.

2. If I were an animal

Close your eyes and take three deep breaths. When you are ready, I'd like you to imagine that you could be any animal you wanted. What would you be?… Why would you like to be this animal?…

Imagine that you *are* this animal… What do you feel like?… What do you like doing?… What do you not like doing?… What is the best thing about being you?… What is the worst thing?… What would you most like to be able to do?…

When you are ready, open your eyes and draw or write about the animal that you chose.

Imagine that!

3. Describing people

These are some words that I can use to describe people.

I can describe how they look (e.g. tall, short, blue eyes, curly hair)

_____   _____   _____

_____   _____   _____

_____   _____   _____

I can describe what they are like (e.g. happy, thoughtful)

_____   _____   _____

_____   _____   _____

_____   _____   _____

4. My group

Write down everyone's name in your class or group. How do you think they would like to be described? Write one friendly describing word next to each name.

5. This is me

Imagine that someone is writing about you for a newspaper. How would you like to be described?

The way I would like to be described is:

_____   _____   _____

_____   _____   _____

_____   _____   _____

_____

6. I am me

Imagine that you are your best friend talking about you. What would your friend say? What might he or she say about what you like doing and what you are good at? What might they say about what you don't like doing and about what worries you? Begin with your name:

_____ is _____

_____

_____

_____

_____

_____

_____

_____

7. Everyone is different

Imagine what it would be like if each of us were exactly the same. Imagine what your family would be like. What about your class or your street or town or the world?! What would be one good thing about everyone being the same?

_____

_____

What would *not* be good about all being the same?

_____

_____

How are you different from your best friend?

_____

_____

8. Something in common?

Sometimes you can find ways that people *are* alike. Find someone in your class or group who is like you in some way.

What is his or her name?

_____

How is this person like you?

_____

Do you know someone who is like you in *lots* of ways? What is his or her name?

_____

How is he or she like you?

_____

_____

This is called 'having something in common'.

9. Making a change

Imagine that a magician could help you to change something about yourself. What would you want to change?

One thing I would like to change is

_____

Close your eyes and imagine that the change you wished for has already happened. How are you different? What is happening now? How do you feel? What would happen next if this change really took place?

_____

_____

_____

_____

_____

10. The change shop

Imagine a shop where you could buy, sell and change things about yourself. Imagine what the shop would look like. Imagine the shop-keeper. What would you sell? What would you like to buy more of? Draw or write about the shop here.

11. Things I like about me

Now think about all the things that you like about yourself and that you would not want to change.

Some things I really like about me are:

_____

_____

_____

_____

_____

_____

_____

12. Important people

Imagine that you are going to tell your class or group about all the people that are important to you. What do you think the other children would like to know?

Draw a picture of one important person and write or draw what he or she likes to do. Why do you think they like to do this?

13. My display cabinet

Imagine that you have a special place where you can put important things on show for everyone to see. Think of some important things about you that you would want to put on display.

An important place for me is

A special fact about me is

An important day was when

My favourite food is

The thing I hate most is

My best friend is called

I would most like to

III
SILVER

Friends and Feelings

You have collected loads of rubies for your treasure chest. Well done! Now we're going hunting for silver while we find out some important things about friends.

It's great to have friends. You can share ideas and worries with them. You can do things together like play computer games, go for walks or just sit and chat.

Sometimes friendships can be difficult too, like when a best friend moves to another town or when you argue about something or you both want to do different things.

Some people seem to make friends very easily. A lot of people find it hard to get to know others who they feel really comfortable with.

With just a little bit of imagination the next part of this book will help you to find out more about friendships.

So – while you collect some silver, let's imagine…

1. Telling people about myself

Imagine that you meet someone for the first time. Think of three things that you could tell them about yourself.

_____

_____

_____

Imagine that you wanted to know about someone else. See if you can think of three things that you could ask them.

_____

_____

_____

2. Finding out a bit more

 Let's imagine that you meet an alien! Think of three things that you would want to ask him.

_____

_____

_____

Now imagine that *you* are the alien. You don't know anything about earth or the people who live here. See if you can think of three things that you would ask.

_____

_____

_____

3. Feelings

What do you think it would feel like to be an alien in a place you didn't know? Think of three words to describe how you would feel if you were an alien.

_____   _____

_____

What are some of the important things you would need to know?

_____

_____

_____

What would help you to feel OK about being in a new place?

_____

_____

4. How many feelings?

Part of getting to know people includes finding out how they are feeling. Our feelings are part of who we are.

There are lots of different words that describe how we feel. Here are just a few:

happy   sad   embarrassed   angry   excited

Write down as many feeling words as you can. Collect some more words from your friends and family by asking them how they are feeling.

_____   _____   _____   _____

_____   _____   _____   _____

_____   _____   _____   _____

_____   _____   _____   _____

5. How I feel

Having a feeling doesn't mean that you are always going to be like that. Jenny might feel shy when she goes to a party where she doesn't know anyone, but that doesn't mean that she is always 'a shy person'. There are lots of times when Jenny feels very confident.

Imagine some times when you have felt some of these feelings. Draw or write about each of the feelings listed on this page.

A time when I felt very brave was

I felt excited when

I felt relaxed when

I felt nervous when

I felt happy when

I felt embarrassed when

6. Imagining that feelings are colours

Simon and Jenny are best friends. They both like to imagine things. Sometimes they use their imaginations to help them to describe how they are feeling.

Today, Simon told Jenny that if he were a colour instead of a person then he would be the colour red because he feels very brave and strong. Jenny said that yesterday she would have been red too because she felt very energetic, but today she would be blue because she feels very calm.

Imagine that you are a colour. Which colour would you be today?

If I were a colour I would be _____

Because _____

Imagine yourself *being* this colour. How do you move as this colour? Do you make a sound? If so, what sound do you make? What do you feel like as this colour?

 Now you are really giving your imagination a good work out!

7. Teasing

Let's spend a little time thinking about something that is not a friendly thing to do. Have you ever been teased?

What is teasing? Think of all the different ways that someone might tease another person.

_____

_____

_____

Think about why people might tease.

_____

_____

_____

8. Getting the picture

Let's carry on str-e-tch-ing our imaginations. If you could get an image of what it's like to be someone who teases others and an image of what it's like to be teased that might help you to understand it even more. Ask your teacher or group leader to read 'teasing' to you.

TEASING

When you're feeling nice and relaxed invite an image to appear in your mind that somehow shows us what it's like to be a person who teases others. This image might be an animal, an object or a plant. Whatever comes into your mind first let that be your image for a person who teases others.

When you have an image spend a little bit of time finding out about it. What can you see when you look at it closely? Does it move? If so, how does it move? Does it make any noise? Now become the image. Step into it and see how it feels to be the image. As the image, ask yourself: 'What is the best thing about being me?... What is the worst thing?' If you could change something about yourself as this image what would you change? What do you want to happen?

Now go back to being yourself again. Take a deep breath and step back into being you. Say goodbye to the image. Relax again.

When you are ready allow an image to come to you that somehow shows what it's like to *be* teased. The first image, that comes into your mind – it might be an object, a plant or an animal. When you have got an image, spend some time finding out what it's like. Look at it from all sides. If you want to, you can become the image for a while. Feel what it is like to *be* this image. What is the best thing about being the image? What is the worst thing? When you are ready, go back to being yourself again. Take a deep breath and step back into being you, just looking at the image.

Now look at both the images together. Imagine that you are an expert on the subject of teasing. If you could give some advice to the two images, what would you say? If you could change something about them or about what is happening what would you do?

Imagine that change happening and see what that is like. What do you want to say to the images now?

When you have finished thank the images and say goodbye to them so that you are ready to gradually come back to feeling more wide awake. When you are ready, draw or write about what you imagined.

9. More on teasing

How does it feel to be teased? Think of as many words as you can to describe what people might feel like when they are teased.

_____

_____

_____

Now let's think of some things that you could do.

If I was being teased I could

_____

_____

_____

If I saw someone else being teased I would

_____

_____

_____

I would not

_____

_____

10. All about my friend

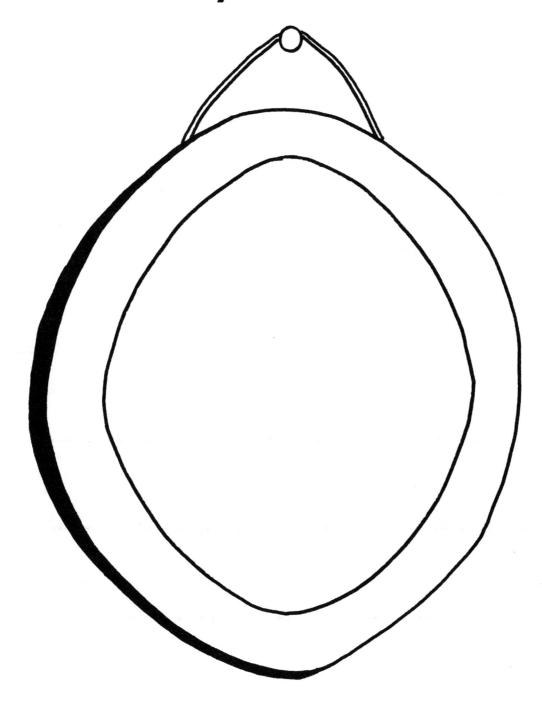

Imagine that one of your friends could look in the magic mirror. What would he see? What would your friend say was important about himself? Draw a picture of your friend in the magic mirror.

11. Recipe for a good friend

Imagine that you have a book full of magic recipes. The very first recipe in the book is how to make friends. What do you think the magic potion will be made of?

_____

_____

_____

_____

_____

12. The house of friendship

Write down all the words about friendships that you can think of. Make sure you write some feeling words as well as some describing words. Write them on the house of friendship.

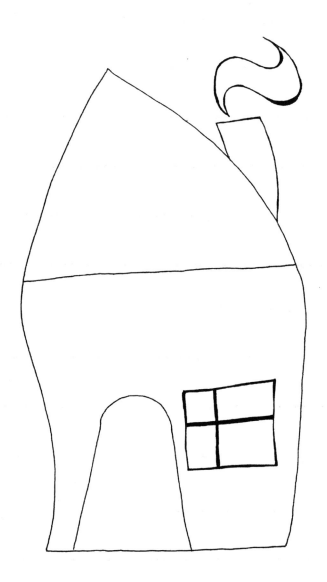

13. What makes a good friend?

_____ is a good friend because

_____

_____

_____

_____

Something we like doing together is

_____

_____

One of the nicest things I have ever done for a friend is

_____

_____

14. Special person for the day

Let's say it's your special day. Everyone is going to be extra specially friendly today. They want to know what you like friends to do so that they can be sure to get it right. What will you tell them?

 I like it when my friends

_____

_____

_____

 It is not friendly to

_____

_____

_____

15. My special friendship day

Imagine that it is the end of your special friendship day and you have had a wonderful time with everyone being extra specially friendly. What did you do together? What did you do that helped the day to go well? What were you like with your friends? (For example, were you relaxed? Smiley?) How did you feel? What do you feel now? Close your eyes and just imagine…

When you are ready draw or write about your special day here.

16. Sharing

What does the word 'sharing' mean?

_____

Imagine that you've just had a birthday and you've been given some special pencils for drawing. You take them into school to use when you do your work. Would it be OK to share them or would that be difficult for you?

If I had some new coloured pencils it would be OK to share them if

_____

It would be hard for me to share them if

_____

What other things can be shared?

_____

_____

_____

_____

17. When being a friend is difficult

Let's say you and your friend disagree about something. Imagine that your friend has come to your house for tea. He or she wants to play outside and you want to play a new game that someone has given to you. How does that feel? What might happen?

Imagine that it is time for your friend to go home now and you didn't manage to sort out the disagreement. How do you feel? What happened? What did you do? What didn't you do?

Now imagine that your friend is going home and you *did* manage to sort things out. You both feel OK. What happened? What did you do? What did you say?

18. More than one

You have had a lot of practice at using images now. Let's think about what it's like to be part of a group.

Close your eyes for a moment so that you can get an image (a plant, an object or an animal) that somehow shows us what a successful group is.

When you have got your image, I'd like you to imagine that you can *become* the image, just like when you imagined being a cat. When you are this image ask yourself 'What is it that makes me work well?' and 'What is the best part of me?'. What do you like about being this image?

When you are ready, draw or write about your image here.

19. The magic mirror

Think about what you have learnt so far.

Look in the magic mirror. What do you see?

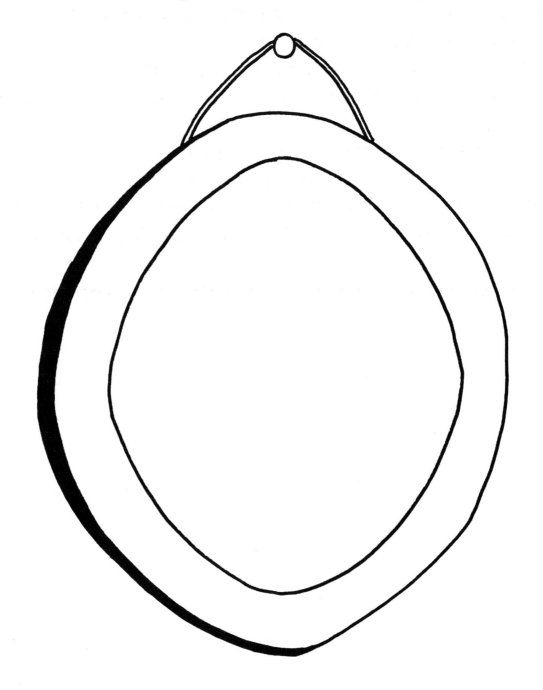

IV
GOLD

Feeling OK about Being Me

Lots of pieces of silver to add to your collection! Your magician's treasure chest is getting more and more full. Now time to look for some gold.

Feeling good about who you are is really important. There are lots of things that happen to us and around us that help us to feel OK about ourselves, but sometimes things happen that are not so nice and we end up feeling bad about ourselves. We might start to think 'I can't do this' or 'I'm no good at this' or 'everyone has more friends than me'.

If this happens then your imagination can help you to feel better about yourself again AND it can help you to actually get to *be* better at doing some of the hard things.

So – let's start collecting gold.

1. Prize-giving day

First of all, let's imagine that it is prize-giving day at the magician's school. Today you will be awarded for ten of the things that you have already achieved. Make a list of the ten things that you would like awards for and then write them in the points of the star.

2. Loads of awards

Imagine being in a big room with all the other apprentice magicians. The chief magician calls out your name and reads out the list of your ten achievements. Everyone claps as you go to receive your awards. What do you get? How do you feel?

Draw or write about your prize-giving day here.

3. Things I'm working on

All through life we are learning new things and often getting better at some of the things we can already do or we already know about. Let's imagine that on prize-giving day at the school for magicians they also give awards for the things that you are working on.

These are the things that you know are a bit difficult for you at the moment so you are working on learning a bit more about them or practising regularly so they'll get easier for you.

Think of five things you are working on and write them here.

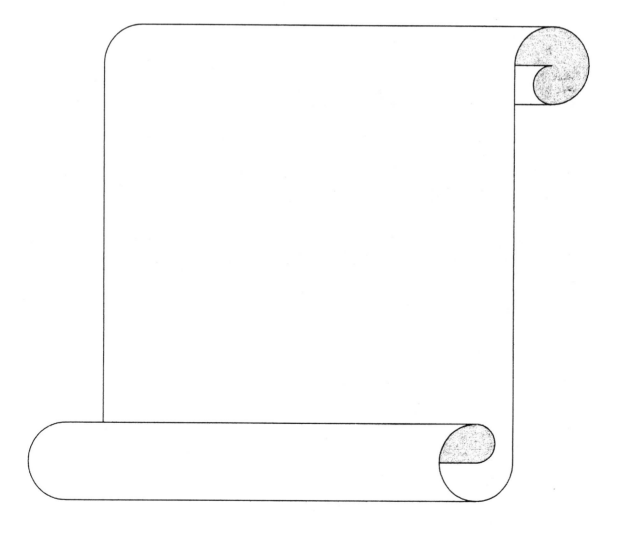

4. More awards

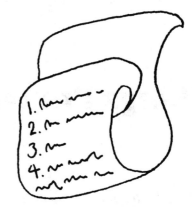

Imagine yourself in the big room again with all the other apprentice magicians. The chief magician calls your name and reads out your list of the five things you are working on. Everyone claps and cheers as you go up to fetch your award. What do you get? How do you feel?

Draw or write about it here.

5. Star turn

Now let's imagine that every person at the school for magicians gets a gold medal for something that they are *really brilliant* at. What will your gold medal be for? Draw a picture or write about something that you are really brilliant at.

6. Confidence

What does the word 'confidence' mean?

_____

_____

Some people can seem to be very confident. Most of us are confident in some things we do and in some places. We have to build up our confidence with other things.

Think about one thing that you would like to be able to do with more confidence.

I would like to be more confident when

_____

_____

_____

7. Let's imagine

Imagine that CONFIDENT is the name of an animal. It could be a real animal or a made-up one. Which animal would it be? See if you can picture it in your mind.

Imagine that you *are* this animal. What do you look like?... How do you move?... What noises do you make?... What does it feel like to be this animal?... What are the nice things about being a CONFIDENT?... Is there anything that is not so nice?... Where do you live?... Who are your friends?... What do you do best?...

When you are ready, draw or write about what it's like to be a CONFIDENT.

8. I felt confident

Now think of a time when you *have* felt confident. Draw or write about it here.

A time when I felt confident was

9. Praise

When someone has done something well or really tried hard with something, they might be praised for it. The good thing about praise is that it can happen at any time and for *lots* of different reasons.

To praise someone means

I can praise people by

When people praise me I feel

Today I praised someone for

Something I would like to be praised for is

10. The magic mirror

Think about what you have learnt while you have been collecting gold.

Look in the magic mirror. What do you see?

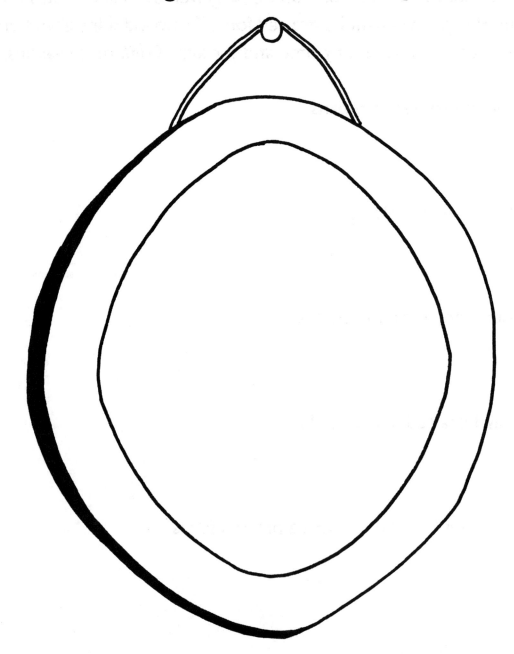

V
PEARLS

Taking Care of Myself

Lots of gold to add to your treasure chest! You're doing really well. Now we go diving for pearls.

With all these things to learn and friends to make and exciting things to do we'd better think about how we take care of ourselves and others.

There are lots of things you can do that will help you to look after yourself.

So – while you are collecting your pearls, let's imagine…

1. Prepare to dive!

When you look after yourself, you feel more ready to enjoy the easy, exciting or fun things in life and more ready to cope with those things that are more difficult.

It's a bit like being ready to go diving in the sea. Take a few minutes to think about what you would need to have with you and what you would need to know if you were going diving; in other words, how you would need to prepare.

Before I go diving I would need to be

_____

_____

I would need to have

_____

_____

I would need to know

_____

_____

2. Feelings

Have you ever worried about something that hasn't happened yet? What did your body feel like? Tick the feelings that you get when you are worried.

butterflies in my tummy ☐   heart beats faster ☐

headache ☐   fidget a lot ☐

feel sick ☐   can't think clearly ☐

tight muscles ☐   wobbly knees ☐

Have you ever got excited about something long before it happened? What did your body feel like then?

_____

_____

_____

Your imagination can make your body feel different things. Sometimes this is good, but sometimes this is not useful for you. Sometimes you might need to change what you are imagining so that you can feel better.

Imagine that!

3. Feeling tense

Think of a time when you felt a bit upset or worried about something. I bet your body felt very stiff and perhaps you felt a bit churned up inside? This is called tension. If tension was an animal or a plant or anything else, what would it be?

Imagine that you can become your image of tension. Step into being this plant or animal or object and feel what it's like.

What does your body feel like? Feel a frown growing from deep inside you. Feel it spreading all the way through you. Really notice what this is like. What is the worst thing about being this image?

Now step out of being this image and back to being you. Give yourself a shake all over…shake your hands, shake your arms, shake your body, shake your legs! Let all that tension disappear.

Draw or write about your image of tension.

4. Feeling relaxed

When we are not tense our body feels more relaxed. If the feeling of relaxing was an animal, a plant or an object, what would it be? Close your eyes and imagine something that somehow shows us what it's like to be relaxed.

When you are ready, draw your image here.

5. Becoming the image

Imagine that you can become your image of relaxation. Step into being this animal or plant or object and really feel what it's like. What does your body feel like?… Feel a smile grow from deep inside you… Feel it spreading all the way through you… Really notice what this is like. What is the best thing about being this image?… Now step out of this image and back to being you.

Think up as many words as you can that tell us what it feels like to be relaxed.

6. Growing happy feelings

Let's imagine that you can grow happy feelings just like you can grow flowers.

Flowers need a lot of looking after to help them to be at their best.

Different flowers need different sorts of earth. Some like shade and some like lots of sun.

Some will only grow where it is very watery and some like to be quite dry.

In the same way, different people would like different things to help them to grow happy feelings. Colour in the flower and write the things that *you* need for your happy feelings to grow.

7. Relaxed breathing

Imagine that your lungs are like balloons. They can get bigger when you fill them with air and then they get smaller again when you let some of the air out.

Sit upright in a chair and put one hand on your stomach. Feel what happens to your stomach when you breathe in and out.

When you think you know what relaxed breathing feels like, see if you can fill in the missing words below.

When I breathe, the air goes in and out of my l _ _ _ _.

I breath in air that is full of o _ _ _ _ _ and this helps to keep my body working well.

When I am relaxed and breathing easily my stomach goes _ _ and _ _ _.

When I breathe in my stomach moves _ _ _ because my l _ _ _ _ are filling up with air.

When I breathe out my stomach goes _ _ because some of the air is going out of my l _ _ _ _.

8a. An image for calm breathing

Calm breathing helps you to feel well and relaxed. It is especially helpful if you have to do something that you are a bit worried about.

Doing some calm breathing before or after (or even during) a difficult time helps your body to relax again.

See if you can work your imagination again.

Imagine this

Close your eyes and ask your imagination to come up with an image that somehow shows us what it's like to have calm breathing. It could be an image of an animal, a plant or an object. Whatever it is, just let it come into your mind.

Now look at the image very closely. Let your imagination look at it from the sides, from the back, from underneath and from the top (as though you are looking down at it). Take your time exploring the image of calm breathing.

Now see if you can *become* your image and really feel what it is like to be the image of calm breathing. Just imagine yourself stepping into your image and becoming it. Take a deep breath and let it go on a sigh. Now ask yourself: 'What is the best thing about being this image?' What can you do as this image?... If you can move, how do you move?... How do you feel now?

Find out as much as you can about your image until you are ready to step back into being you... You can leave the image now. Thank your imagination for showing this to you. Let the image fade away.

Open your eyes and, when you are ready, draw or write about your image.

8b. My image of calm breathing

Remember that whenever you are feeling a bit tense or worried, thinking of this image will help you to relax a little bit and to have the calm breathing that you need.

9. Taking care of myself every day

Imagine that you've had a very busy day at school and you feel quite tired. Think of all the things that you could do now to help yourself to feel relaxed and refreshed. Draw or write about them here.

Ask at least three other people what they like doing to help themselves to relax. Write or draw their answers here.

10. How to make a perfect day

Let's go back to the magician's recipe book again and think about how to make a perfect day for ourselves.

What ingredients would you need for *your* perfect day?

_____

_____

_____

_____

Imagine that you have *had* the most perfect day. Describe what happened.

_____

_____

_____

_____

11. Letting go of worries

Imagine that there is a tree called the HugMe tree. It is so big and has so many branches that it can take all your worries for you. Draw or write about any worries you might have and hang them on the branches. You can use the HugMe tree at night to hang up your worries before you go to sleep. Just picture it in your mind.

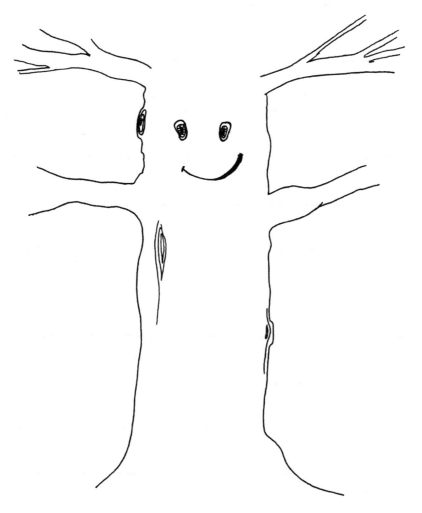

Imagine yourself giving the HugMe tree a great big hug!

12. Any more worries?

Imagine that you could post your worries into a worry box.

What do you think should happen to them then? Where would they go? Would anyone look at them? If so, who would it be? What would they do with them? Draw or write about what happens.

Imagine that!

13. The worry team

Imagine that you are part of a worry team. This is a group of exceptionally clever people who spend their time inventing ways of getting rid of worries. They thought of the HugMe tree and the worry box. Make a list of other things that you could do with worries. How inventive can you be?

14. The magic mirror

Think about what you have learnt while you've been diving for pearls.

Look in the magic mirror. What do you see?

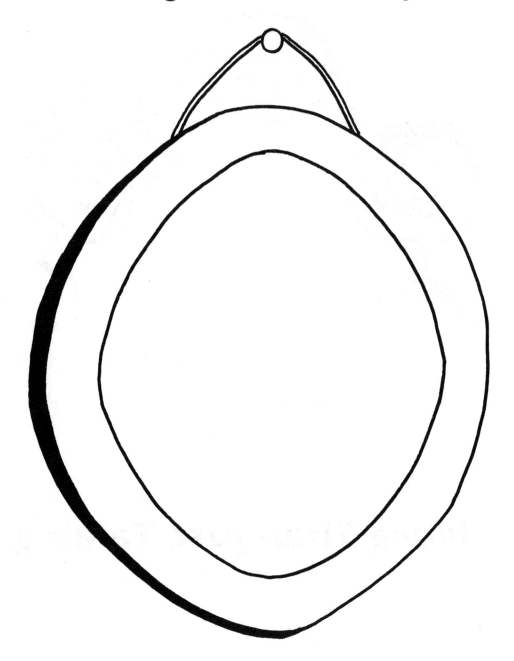

VI
SAPPHIRES

More Than Just Talking

Well you seem to have things under control in the worry department! You have plenty of pearls brought up from the sea.

The next treasure to hunt for is a pocketful of sapphires.

Lots of people have difficulty with their talking. Perhaps you have some difficulty (like stuttering) or you know of someone else who does.

Even if you don't struggle with your speaking, perhaps there are times when you feel a bit anxious about having to give a talk in front of your class or group or when you are taking part in a play or a school assembly.

The next bit of the magician's book tells you all about how we communicate with each other.

There is much more to communicating than just talking – and a lot of beautiful sapphires to collect while you learn all about it!

1. All about how we talk

When you talk you use different parts of your mouth and throat to make speech sounds. Sounds go together to make words and words can go together to make sentences. Everyone sounds different when they talk because we all have different-shaped mouths and throats and we move our speech muscles in slightly different ways. See if you can find out the names of some of the parts of the body that we use when we speak.

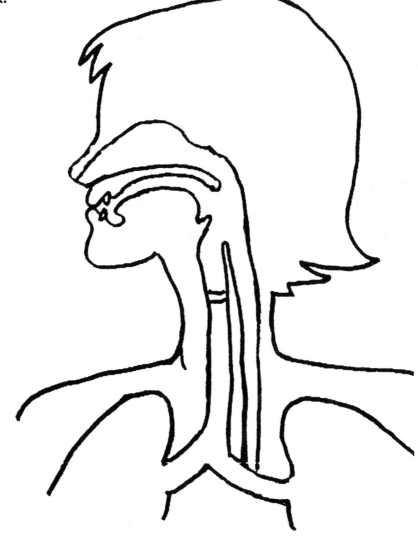

2. Conversations

What does the word 'conversation' mean?

Draw a picture or write about a conversation you have had today. Who were you talking with? Who started the conversation? What was the conversation about? Who did the most talking? Who did the most listening? How did the conversation end?

3. Talking skills

When we talk to each other we do lots of different things that help to make what we say clear and easy to understand.

Let's imagine

Imagine that you are watching television. You are watching a programme about the two friends, Simon and Jenny. They are having a conversation about the day they went on a school trip together. What are they doing when they talk to each other? Where are they looking? How do they sound? Do they both talk at the same time?

See if you can fill the speech box with lots of words to describe good talking skills.

4. Listening skills

Do you think that listening is the same as hearing?

Imagine that you are walking in a busy town with someone in your family. Draw or write all the things that you imagine yourself hearing.

Now put a circle around the things you would actually listen to. Can you listen to more than one thing at the same time?

5a. Let's imagine

Mike and Bill

Mike and Bill are best friends. Bill is very good at talking to other people but Mike makes lots of mistakes. See if you can spot all the mistakes that Mike makes in this story.

One day Mike was mending his skateboard outside his house when Bill walked by. Mike heard Bill's footsteps and looked up. Bill waved and said, 'Hi Mike!' Mike looked back at his skateboard and carried on trying to fix the wheel.

'What are you doing?' asked Bill, kneeling down beside Mike.

'My Dad gave it to me,' said Mike. 'I think he's at work.'

'It's a great looking skateboard,' said Bill. 'How did the wheel come off?'

Mike didn't answer so Bill carried on talking.

'I used to have a skateboard but it broke when my brother tried to race it down a steep hill and it crashed into a tree at the bottom. I was really fed up and...'

'Sally isn't at home so that means we can have fish pie for tea,' Mike said suddenly.

Bill pulled a face. He wrinkled his nose and curled his lips as though he'd tasted something really disgusting. 'Oh I *love* fish pie,' he said.

'Do you?' asked Mike, not looking up.

'No 'course not…can't stand it,' replied Bill. 'And anyway, what's fish pie got to do with Sally?'

But Mike had fixed the wheel on his skateboard and was ready to try it out. 'Bye then,' called Bill. 'See you at school tomorrow.'

'I wonder if Bill's got that new computer game yet,' thought Mike as he whizzed down the path on his board.

5b Mike and Bill

How many mistakes did you spot? Write them down here.

6. Taking turns

What do we mean when we talk about 'taking turns'?

_____

Why is it important to take turns when we talk to each other?

_____

What would happen if we didn't take turns when we talked to each other? Imagine yourself having a conversation with some friends. Imagine that they are talking so much that you don't get a chance to say anything. What do you feel? What happens? What would you like to do?

_____

_____

_____

_____

_____

7. Looking

Why is it important to look at each other when we are talking?

_____

Who does the most looking? Is it the person who is speaking or the person who is listening?

_____

Imagine what it feels like when the person you are talking to isn't looking at you.

_____

Imagine that you are talking to your friends and you are looking down at the floor. Imagine what your friends might be thinking.

_____

_____

_____

_____

_____

8. Keeping good eye contact

If people are able to look at each other easily when they are talking and listening it is called 'keeping good eye contact'. Lots of people find this very difficult to do, especially if they are feeling a bit shy.

Keeping good eye contact is an important part of feeling and looking confident. So now you're going to put your imagination to work by thinking up some games for practising eye contact.

Draw or write about your games here.

9. Body talk

Sometimes it is possible to know how someone is feeling even before they say anything. They *show* us how they feel by the way they are standing or sitting and by the expression on their face.

What do you think the person in this picture is feeling?

Let's imagine

Close your eyes and imagine what he would look like if he was happy. How would he stand? Do you think he would be moving his hands or would they be still? What would his face be like? Make as clear a picture as possible in your mind. Now imagine what he would look like if he was nervous. What about if he was sad? When you are ready, see if you can draw or write about the things that happen when we use our bodies to talk.

10. How do we sound when we talk?

People talk in lots of different ways. Some people talk very fast. Some people talk quite slowly. Some people have a high voice and some talk with a very low, deep-sounding voice. Perhaps you've heard people talking in a different language to yours or with a different accent?

Now and then we all have difficulty getting our words out. Write the words 'my cat is black and white' in the speech bubbles and show what different speech mistakes can sound like. We might mix our words up by mistake. What do you think that might sound like?

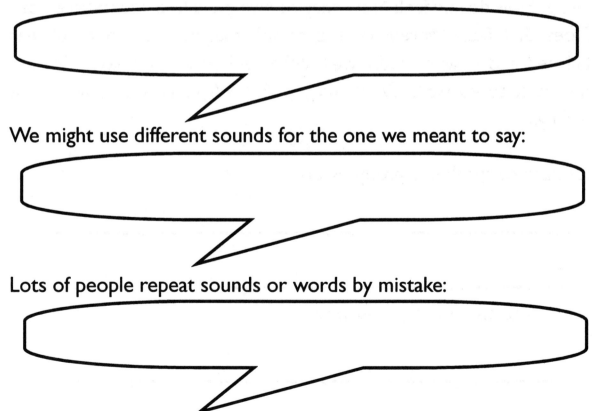

We might use different sounds for the one we meant to say:

Lots of people repeat sounds or words by mistake:

All these different ways of talking can happen to all of us a little bit and to some of us a lot.

11. Speaking in a group

Talking to just one person sometimes feels different from talking in a group so let's think about this a bit more.

Let's imagine

Imagine that you are with some friends and you are telling them about something that you did yesterday. Where do you imagine yourself being? How do you feel? Now imagine giving a talk to your whole class. Does that feel different or the same? Imagine that your talk has finished and it went really well. What did your classmates do that helped it to go well? What did *you* do? Write about some of the feelings.

It's hard to speak in a group when

_____

_____

It's easy to speak in a group when

_____

_____

12. What I feel about speaking in a group

If I were going to speak in a group it would be OK if

_____

_____

_____

_____

It would be difficult for me if

_____

_____

_____

_____

13. What I like about the way I talk

Think about your own talking now. Think about all the things that you do when you talk, as well as how you sound.

Imagine that you have just had a long conversation with a friend. Write a list of all the things that you did to help the conversation to go well.

I imagined that I was talking to _____

This is what I did to help it to go well

_____

_____

_____

_____

_____

14. The magic mirror

Think about what you have found out while you have been collecting sapphires.

Look in the magic mirror. What do you see?

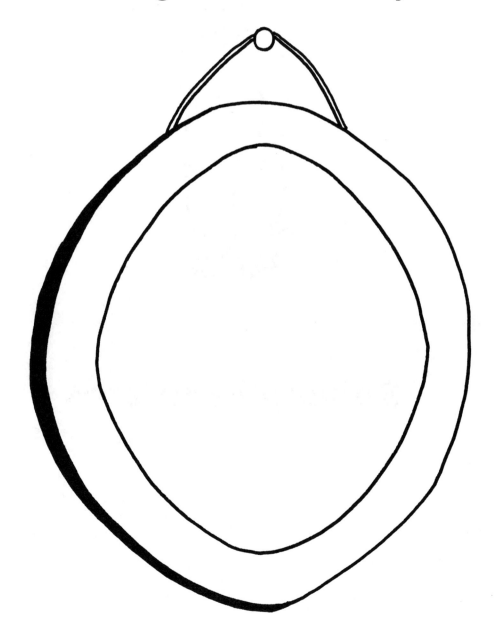

VII
RAINBOWS

Solving Problems

Keep those sapphires safe while we hunt for rainbows!

As you learn new things you get better and better at solving problems. For example, maybe you wouldn't know how to untangle a knot in your shoelaces unless you knew how to tie a knot in the first place.

Problems to be solved come in all shapes and sizes. Sometimes we have little problems to solve (like untying knots) and sometimes we have bigger problems (like what to do if our best friend doesn't want to play with us).

Sometimes we have problems that just seem too huge for us to solve on our own.

So, next we're going to look at how we can help ourselves to solve problems.

1. Let's imagine

Imagine if problems were animals or plants or anything at all that could be drawn. What would they be? Fill this page up with drawings that somehow show us what little problems and medium-sized problems and really big problems are like.

2a. A problem shared

Choose one of your pictures and give it a name. For example, 'friend problem' or 'homework problem' or 'maths problem'.

Let's imagine

Look at what you have drawn and imagine yourself becoming the image – just to see what it is like. When you pretend that you are this image, what does that feel like? Do you feel big and strong, or small and not very strong at all?

What colour are you? If you can move, how do you move?

Problems like to be solved! As this problem, what would you like to happen now?

When you are ready, step out of being your image problem and go back to being you again.

Was the problem the size you expected it to be? What did you find out?

Draw your problem again now that you know a bit more about it.

2b. Problem talk

If you could talk to your image problem now what would you want to say to it? What does it say back to you? Imagine yourself having a conversation with it.

Do you want to ask it to do anything?

When you are ready, write about what happened.

2c. Where has it gone?

Now imagine the *opposite* of the problem you chose. What does this look like? Imagine its colour, how it feels to touch, its size and weight.
    Draw the opposite of the problem here.

2d. Something changes

Now draw a third picture. Fill the whole page with a picture that somehow shows us how your problem image is going to change.

If this picture somehow showed us a solution (an answer) to your problem what would that solution be?

_____

2e. Making it happen

How can you help this change to happen in real life? What is the first small thing that you could do that would help?

If I want to solve this problem I could

_____

_____

_____

_____

_____

_____

Imagine that!

3. One less problem

Think of a time when you solved a problem on your own. Draw or write about it here.

4. Still puzzled?

Sometimes we meet problems that we just don't understand at all. It's as if the problem came from another planet!

Think about what you need to do if you come across something that you don't understand.

If I don't understand something I could

_____

_____

_____

_____

5. A bit of magical wisdom

Let's imagine... THE BOOK OF WISDOM

Imagine that you have a special book. A book that knows the answer to lots of different questions. It is especially good at solving problems. When you talk to this book it always listens and sooner or later it always comes up with an answer.

If you have a question or a problem to solve write or draw about it here.

Close your eyes and imagine that you can ask the Book of Wisdom to help you. What does it tell you? Write or draw what it says.

Sometimes, the answer doesn't come straightaway. Sometimes you have to wait a few days and then – just when you least expect it, you'll find the answer!

6. The magic mirror

What have you found out about yourself while you searched for rainbows?

Look in the magic mirror. What do you see?

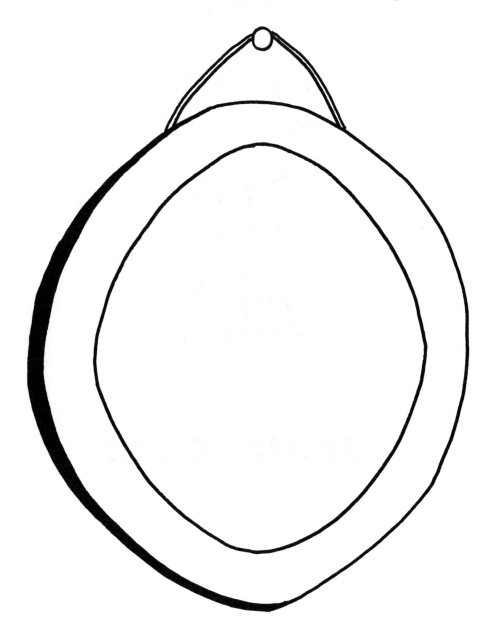

VIII
MOONBEAMS

Setting Goals

Now you've almost finished collecting treasure. While you've been drawing and writing and imagining, you've also learnt lots about yourself and about other people.

Now all that's needed is for you to take some time to set some goals for yourself. You can think of these as 'targets' – things that you would like to achieve in the future.

We know that the people who have most fun in life and who feel good about themselves are the ones who set themselves small targets every so often.

Sometimes they set themselves big targets as well!

It's up to you what you want to achieve for yourself.

In these last few pages I'd like you to imagine that you are collecting moonbeams while you go on a journey into space.

1a. Taking off

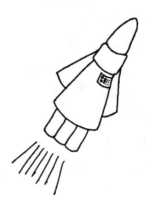

Let's imagine

Let's imagine that you can travel into the future in your own special spaceship. What sort of a spaceship is it? Is there room for two people inside or just enough for one? Imagine that you can step into the spaceship.

Have a look at the controls. There are lots of them. There's a button that has a sign under it saying 'to the stars'. When you're ready to go all you have to do is press this button and the spaceship will gently take off and head up into the sky. Ready?

Your spaceship takes you through the clouds. The sky around you is becoming a deeper and deeper blue and you can see the stars shining ahead of you. You're going high into the place where everything and anything is possible.

Somewhere up here is your own special star and the spaceship is going to take you right up close to it so you can see it really well.

Notice all the little details about this very special star as the spaceship hovers near it and circles around it.

If there is something you have to get done or a goal you want to set for yourself then this is the star that will be able to show you what it will be like for you once you've achieved it.

1b. Just the right star

Draw your star here.

Imagine that there is a beam of light shining out from the star into the sky. It can project pictures on the sky as though you were at the cinema.

As you watch you can see a big screen forming in the sky ahead of you. On to this screen walks a person…it's you! This is you after you've achieved your goal.

What do you look like on the screen? What is the 'future you' doing? What did you do to make this happen? What did you need to have or to know so that you could achieve your goal? How is 'you' on the screen different from you sitting in the spaceship?

The future you says goodbye and is walking away now. As you watch, the beam of light from the star starts to get fainter and the screen starts to fade until eventually it has disappeared altogether.

Time now to leave the stars. Take one last look around. Press the button that says 'home' and away goes the spaceship, through the deep blue sky…through the floating clouds…slowly and gently back down to the ground.

As you get out of the spaceship notice if you feel any different now to how you felt when you first set off.

When you are ready write a letter to yourself from the future, telling yourself how to work on your goal.

2. A letter to myself

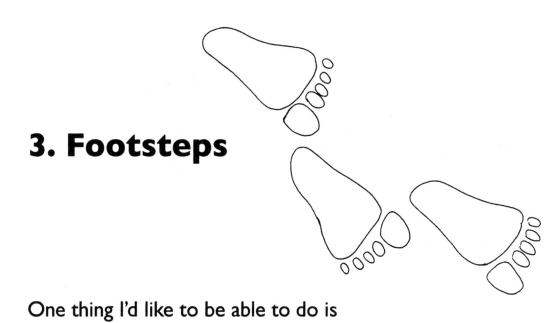

3. Footsteps

One thing I'd like to be able to do is

_____

These are the steps I need to take

4. If I were famous

I would like to be famous for

_____

_____

_____

_____

_____

5. Recipe for success

I will succeed if

_____

_____

_____

_____

_____

_____

_____

6. My treasure chest

Let's imagine that your treasure chest is now full of all the wonderful things about being you. Can you imagine the chest? What is it made of? How big is it?

Imagine that every bit of treasure somehow shows us something special about you. Each piece of treasure has a label on it to show us what it is.

It would be a shame to keep all that treasure shut away in the chest all the time don't you think?

Imagine that every day you go to your treasure chest and take a few things out to put on show so that we can all admire it.

What treasure will you choose today?

From my treasure chest today I chose

_____

_____

_____

_____

7. GOAL RECORD SHEET

My goal is _____

_____

I tried it when _____

This is what happened _____

_____

_____

The next thing I'm going to try is _____

_____

_____

_____

_____

8. I can change the way that I feel about myself by doing these things:

_____ ☐

_____ ☐

_____ ☐

_____ ☐

_____ ☐

_____ ☐

_____ ☐

_____ ☐

Put a tick in each box when you have achieved the goals that you decide on.

9. The magic mirror

Think about what you have learnt while you have been collecting moonbeams.

Look in the magic mirror. What do you see?

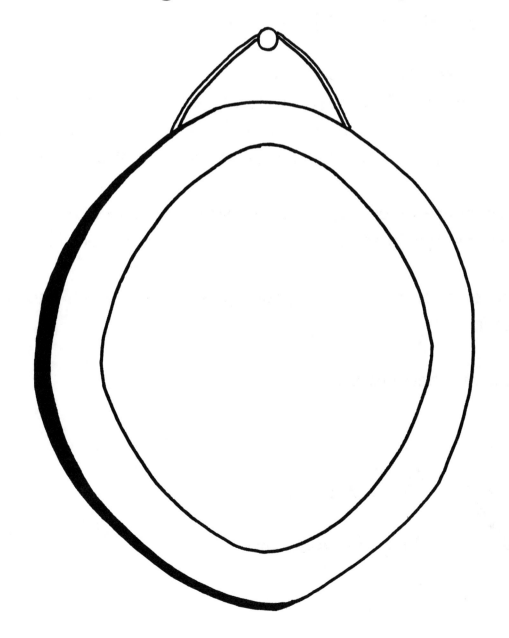

Dear Magician,

Congratulations! You have now collected all the treasure that you need for your magician's treasure chest.

Remember that it is important that you feel good about yourself, no matter what difficulties you have to deal with. Remember too that even qualified magicians make mistakes sometimes. This is all part of how we carry on learning about ourselves and about other people.

You have used your imagination to learn all sorts of things already, and you know that imagination is free and it's always there for you!

Now that you have this magician's power, use it wisely and have fun with it.

With very best wishes,

Deborah

(Magician's Assistant)

Sample Checklist and Progress Record

Name: Date of Birth:

Skill	Rating		Comments	Aims
	pre	post		
Keeps appropriate level of eye contact with peers when talking/listening				
Keeps appropriate level of eye contact with adults when talking/listening				
Can tolerate own mistakes and accept constructive criticism				
Volunteers answers in whole-class discussions (literacy/science)				
Volunteers short answers in whole-class activities (e.g. maths)				
Can successfully engage in co-operative games/activities				

Asks appropriate adult for help when needed				
Initiates conversation with peers				
Initiates conversation with adults				
Can put forward own views and be assertive in interactions with peers				
Can describe own feelings and those of others				
Achieves at or near academic potential				
Recognises own abilities and qualities				

RATING SCALE

Examples:

1 = Child finds this very difficult in all situations

5 = Child has some difficulty in some situations

10 = Child has no difficulty with this in any situation

Signs of Possible Low Self-Esteem and/or Anxiety

- Poor posture (e.g. shoulders drooped or tense)
- Avoids eye contact
- Picks at clothes; chews cuffs or sleeves
- Chews lip
- Bites fingernails
- Stays close to adult (e.g. member of staff) at playtime
- Observes group games from sidelines
- Flat affect (rarely shows emotion)
- Tearful
- Complains of physical symptoms (e.g. stomach-ache, headache)
- Does not complete set work or completes it hurriedly (below known potential)
- Frequently teases or bullies others
- Is a frequent victim of teasing or bullying
- Frequently absent from school
- Difficulty in concentrating
- Easily influenced by peers
- May be verbally aggressive or withdrawn or alternate unpredictably between these

Adult Behaviour That Supports Self-Esteem in Children

giving time

loving   trusting

listening   having realistic expectations

describing actions (not labelling behaviour)

making positive requests
(defining the appropriate behaviour)

acknowledging   accepting

respecting   rewarding

encouraging   celebrating achievements

negotiating

modelling appropriate behaviour

giving responsibility   empathizing

shared problem-solving

defining appropriate boundaries

giving unqualified praise

Building Your Own Self-Esteem

There are many excellent books on self-esteem for adults. These are just a few 'key' points to take into consideration.

- Make time for yourself. You are important.
- Set regular short-term goals as well as long-term goals. Make sure they are realistic and attainable.
- Make sure any self-criticism is CONSTRUCTIVE not DESTRUCTIVE.
- Be ready to accept constructive criticism from others and to cope with unjustified criticism in an assertive way.
- Own your own feelings. Don't assume that others *know* what you are feeling.
- Use 'I' statements, such as 'I am angry' not 'You make me angry'.
- Be able to forgive yourself for past mistakes.
- Acknowledge your successes and reward yourself.
- Be proud of who you are and what you achieve.
- Accept sincere compliments and praise from others.
- Resolve to eliminate self-defeating phrases from your speech.
- Learn the skill of being your own friend.

Appendix E

Relaxation Script

This type of relaxation works by focusing the mind on different areas of the body and just being aware of what that area feels like. Often if we try to relax, we try too hard! In our efforts to relax we actually set up more tension. By observing what the body is doing there is inevitably a natural tendency simply to allow any areas of tension to relax and release. This relaxation can be done lying down or seated. Read the instructions very slowly and calmly with plenty of pauses to allow the children time to follow your instructions.

Sometimes if we are very anxious or nervous or tense about something it shows in our body. Our muscles become tight. Maybe they begin to ache a little bit. We might feel 'knotted up' inside. It's really good to learn how to relax your body so that you can feel better, feel more confident, feel more able to do those things that are sometimes a bit difficult for you.

When you are ready, let your eyes close gently and settle yourself into a comfortable position.

I'd like you to think about your right foot and just notice what it feels like. It might be warm or cold. It might be numb or itchy. It might be tight or relaxed. Just notice whatever you can feel right now in your right foot… Now gently move your attention from your right foot to the lower part of your right leg. Let your thoughts leave your right foot and just move very easily to your right leg. Notice whatever feeling is there just at this moment… There are no right or wrong feelings… Whatever you can feel is OK… Now move up to your knee…and then the top part of your right leg and notice whatever feelings are there… Now to your right hand. Feel what's happening in your right hand… Notice all the fingers of your right hand. They might feel cool or warm, numb or itchy, tight or relaxed. Just notice whatever is there. Now think about your right arm and feel what's happening there… Whatever is there, just notice it…

Now go across your body now to the top part of your left arm… Now down through your elbow to the bottom half of your left arm… And now your left hand and fingers… Now the top half of your left leg. Notice whatever is happening there… And then from your knee down to your ankle… And now down into your left foot… Now notice both your legs and both your feet at the same time… Really notice what they feel like… Now notice your arms and hands as well as your legs and feet…

Now start to notice the rest of your body as well... Notice your tummy and your chest... Notice your back and your shoulders... Notice all the feelings around your neck and your head...

Now, instead of thinking of yourself in parts, feel your whole body relax. Just letting go of any last little bits of tightness. As you breathe in, breathe in relaxation... As you breathe out, breathe away the tightness... Lie quietly for a few moments and enjoy the feeling of being relaxed...

Keep noticing your body and start to listen to whatever sounds there are around you... Begin to move your hands and feet a little bit... When you feel ready, open your eyes and look around you... Lie or sit quietly for a short while before stretching and slowly getting up...

Children's Storybooks to Read

(6–8 year olds)

A Treasury of Stories for Eight Year Olds chosen by Edward and Nancy Blishen (Kingfisher, 1995)

And to Think That I Saw It on Mulberry Street by Dr Seuss (HarperCollins, 1992)

Bill's New Frock by Anne Fine (Mammoth Books, 1999)

Daisy-Head Mayzie by Dr Seuss (HarperCollins Children's Books, 1996)

Friends and Brothers by Dick King-Smith (Mammoth Books, 1999)

Fergus the Forgetful by Margaret Ryan and Wendy Smith (Collins, 1995)

Horton Hatches the Egg by Dr Seuss (HarperCollins Children's Books, 1998)

I Had Trouble in Getting to Solla Sollew by Dr Seuss (HarperCollins Children's Books, 1998)

I'm Scared by Bel Money (Mammoth Books, 1998)

I'm Worried by Brian Moses (Wayland Publishers, 1997)

Nothing by Mick Inkpen (Hodder Children's Books, 1996)

Only a Show by Anne Fine (Puffin Books, 1998)

Scaredy Cat by Anne Fine (Mammoth Books, 1998)

Something Else by Kathryn Cave and Chris Riddell (Picture Puffins, 1995)

The Huge Bag of Worries by Virginia Ironside (Macdonald Young Books, 1998)

The Lighthouse Keeper's Lunch by Ronda and David Armitage (Scholastic Children's Books, 1994)

The Selfish Crocodile by Faustin Charles and Michael Terry (Bloomsbury Children's Books, 1999)

Subject Index

Activities Index